JULIAN BOND

The African-American Biographies Series

MARIAN ANDERSON
Singer and Humanitarian
0-7660-1211-5

MAYA ANGELOU
More Than a Poet
0-89490-684-4

LOUIS ARMSTRONG
King of Jazz
0-89490-997-5

ARTHUR ASHE
Breaking the Color Barrier
in Tennis
0-89490-689-5

BENJAMIN BANNEKER
Astronomer and Mathematician
0-7660-1208-5

JULIAN BOND
Civil Rights Activist and Chairman of the NAACP
0-7660-1549-1

RALPH BUNCHE
Winner of the Nobel Peace Prize
0-7660-1203-4

BESSIE COLEMAN
First Black Woman Pilot
0-7660-1545-9

W. E. B. DU BOIS
Champion of Civil Rights
0-7660-1209-3

PAUL LAURENCE DUNBAR
Portrait of a Poet
0-7660-1350-2

DUKE ELLINGTON
Giant of Jazz
0-89490-691-7

ARETHA FRANKLIN
Motown Superstar
0-89490-686-0

NIKKI GIOVANNI
Poet of the People
0-7660-1238-7

WHOOPI GOLDBERG
Comedian and Movie Star
0-7660-1205-0

LORRAINE HANSBERRY
Playwright and Voice of Justice
0-89490-945-2

MATTHEW HENSON
Co-Discoverer of the North Pole
0-7660-1546-7

LANGSTON HUGHES
Poet of the Harlem Renaissance
0-89490-815-4

ZORA NEALE HURSTON
Southern Storyteller
0-89490-685-2

JESSE JACKSON
Civil Rights Activist
0-7660-1390-1

QUINCY JONES
Musician, Composer, Producer
0-89490-814-6

BARBARA JORDAN
Congresswoman, Lawyer,
Educator
0-89490-692-5

CORETTA SCOTT KING
Striving for Civil Rights
0-89490-811-1

MARTIN LUTHER KING, JR.
Leader for Civil Rights
0-89490-687-9

KWEISI MFUME
Congressman and NAACP Leader
0-7660-1237-9

TONI MORRISON
Nobel Prize-Winning Author
0-89490-688-7

WALTER DEAN MYERS
Writer for Real Teens
0-7660-1206-9

JESSE OWENS
Track and Field Legend
0-89490-812-X

COLIN POWELL
Soldier and Patriot
0-89490-810-3

A. PHILIP RANDOLPH
Union Leader and Civil Rights Crusader
0-7660-1544-0

PAUL ROBESON
Actor, Singer, Political Activist
0-89490-944-4

JACKIE ROBINSON
Baseball's Civil Rights Legend
0-89490-690-9

BETTY SHABAZZ
Sharing the Vision
of Malcolm X
0-7660-1210-7

HARRIET TUBMAN
Moses of the Underground Railroad
0-7660-1548-3

MADAM C. J. WALKER
Self-Made Businesswoman
0-7660-1204-2

IDA B. WELLS-BARNETT
Crusader Against Lynching
0-89490-947-9

OPRAH WINFREY
Talk Show Legend
0-7660-1207-7

CARTER G. WOODSON
Father of African-American History
0-89490-946-0

—African-American Biographies—

JULIAN BOND

Civil Rights Activist and Chairman of the NAACP

Series Consultant:
Dr. Russell L. Adams, Chairman
Department of Afro-American Studies, Howard University

Denise M. Jordan

Enslow Publishers, Inc.

40 Industrial Road   PO Box 38
Box 398   Aldershot
Berkeley Heights, NJ 07922   Hants GU12 6BP
USA   UK

http://www.enslow.com

Library of Congress Cataloging-in-Publication Data

Jordan, Denise.
    Julian Bond, civil rights activist and chairman of the NAACP / by Denise M. Jordan.
        p. cm. — (African-American biographies)
    Includes bibliographical references and index.
    ISBN 0-7660-1549-1
      1. Bond, Julian, 1940—Juvenile literature. 2. African American legislators—Georgia—Biography—Juvenile literature. 3. Legislators—Georgia—Biography—Juvenile literature. 4. African American civil rights workers—Biography—Juvenile literature. 5. National Association for the Advancement of Colored People—Biography—Juvenile literature.
6. African Americans—Civil rights—Georgia—History—20th century—Juvenile literature. 7. African Americans—Civil rights—History—20th century—Juvenile literature. 8. Georgia—Politics and government—1951—Juvenile literature. [1. Bond, Julian, 1940–   . 2. legislators. 3. Civil rights workers. 4. African Americans—Biography.]
    I. Title. II. Series.
      F291.3.B66 J67   2001
      323.1'196073'0092—dc21

                             00-012423

Printed in the United States of America

10 9 8 7 6 5 4 3 2 1

To Our Readers:
We have done our best to make sure all Internet addresses in this book were active and appropriate when we went to press. However, the author and the publisher have no control over and assume no liability for the material available on those Internet sites or on other Web sites they may link to. Any comments or suggestions can be sent by e-mail to comments@enslow.com or to the address on the back cover.

Every effort has been made to locate all copyright holders of material used in this book. If any errors or omissions have occurred, corrections will be made in future editions of this book.

Illustration Credits: Courtesy of George School, pp. 25, 100, 103; Courtesy of Julian Bond, pp. 6, 14, 17, 33, 85; Courtesy of the Atlanta History Center, pp. 66, 73, 76, 86, 89, 91; Courtesy of the Atlanta University Center, Robert W. Woodruff Library, p. 80; Courtesy of Willie E. Jordan, pp. 107, 112; Morehouse College, Office of Alumni Relations, Atlanta, Georgia, pp. 40, 47, 59, 94; Special Collections Department, Pullen Library, Georgia State University, p. 56.

Cover Credit: Courtesy of Julian Bond.

CONTENTS

Julian Bond

1

"THE INFAMOUS MR. BOND"

ulian Bond and several other college students climbed the long flight of steps to the gallery in the Georgia Statehouse. The 1961 Georgia General Assembly was in session. Bond and the others from Morehouse College and Spelman College wanted to observe state government in action.

They paused outside the door to read the signs. One section of the gallery was marked "Colored" and another section was marked "Whites Only." The students looked at one another, whispered a few words, then walked inside. They bypassed the colored section and made their way into the whites-only section of the gallery.

Suddenly all business on the House floor stopped. A loud booming voice called out, "Mr. Speak-ah! Git those [Negroes] out of the white section of the gallery!"[1]

Doors opened and state troopers came rushing in. Bond and his peers took off at a fast clip, exiting the gallery. They walked quickly back down the hall, down the long staircase, and out the door into the Georgia sunshine. The state police followed to make sure they left the building.

Five years later, in 1966, Julian Bond was in the Georgia Statehouse again. He was there to be sworn in as a member of the Georgia House of Representatives. As the elected statesmen stood for the swearing-in ceremony, Bond was asked to step aside. Seventy-five petitions had been filed against his right to take the oath of office. The other new representatives were sworn in, but Bond was not. Once again, he was thrown out of the statehouse.

Bond had angered a number of people when he made statements opposing the Vietnam War. These people accused him of treason. They believed that speaking out against the war was wrong. To punish Bond, veteran House members started a drive to keep him out of the Georgia House of Representatives.

Bond took his battle to court. He had been elected

to the office and believed he was entitled to hold it. In a press conference, Bond said, "Negroes have died for the right to vote in Georgia. Now they are saying, what good does it do to get the vote, to elect representatives, if those elected must face 'attitude tests' and loyalty oaths?"[2] Bond was determined to take his place in the Georgia House.

Three times Bond ran for and won his House seat. He went to court twice, filing first in the federal district court, then in the United States Supreme Court. On December 5, 1966, the Supreme Court voted unanimously that Julian Bond had been treated unfairly. His rights to free speech, clearly defined in the First Amendment to the Constitution, had been violated. The Court ruled that the members of the Georgia House must seat Julian Bond.

Julian Bond fought for what he believed in, and he won. This was just one of many battles he was to fight for civil rights and equal opportunities for African-American people.

2

GROWING UP

I t was January 14, 1940, and Dr. Horace Mann Bond was awaiting the birth of his second child. His wife, Julia Washington Bond, had gone into labor at their home in Fort Valley, Georgia, several hours earlier. Mrs. Bond did not want to have her baby in the poorly equipped clinic available to blacks near Fort Valley. She insisted that Dr. Bond drive her to Hubbard Hospital in Nashville, Tennessee.[1]

Hubbard Hospital was a part of Meharry Medical College, a black college in Nashville. Mrs. Bond had been raised in Nashville; she was familiar with the people and the place. She wanted to go home. After driving frantically to the hospital, Dr. Bond waited. Finally, he was given the news that his wife had safely delivered a boy. They named him Horace Julian Bond.

The Bonds named their baby after his father, Horace Mann Bond II. To distinguish between father and son, the baby was called Julian. The Bonds already had a one-year-old daughter, Jane.

Dr. Bond held a doctoral degree in education. He was well known as a scholar, an educator, and an administrator. When Julian was born, Dr. Bond was president of Fort Valley State College, a black college located in Georgia.

Young Julian grew up in a family that emphasized learning. Dr. Bond had done research on intelligence testing and black students. He believed that a child's intelligence was not just due to heredity. The environment and early stimulation of the child were more important. In support of his beliefs, the Bonds tacked large printed words on the walls of the playroom and taped others to the crib so that Julian could learn to read them.[2]

Julian's mother, a graduate of Fisk University, had been a librarian. She gave up her job to do the entertaining necessary for the wife of a college administrator and to raise her children. She, too, believed in the value of books and the importance of reading. She read to the children often, taught them to pick out words, and corrected their pronunciation.

Julian Bond later said, "One thing my parents did for me above everything else was to encourage me to read. They taught me how to read when I was four."[3]

Many influential people visited the Bond home. One of these people was the well-known writer, educator, and civil rights activist W. E. B. Du Bois. Du Bois was a founder of the National Association for the Advancement of Colored People (NAACP); editor of *Crisis*, the official magazine of the NAACP; and chairman of the sociology department of Atlanta University. Dr. Bond had written and submitted articles to *Crisis*, and the men knew each other from collegiate circles. What began as a professional relationship grew into a lasting friendship.

Du Bois traveled around the South speaking on racial issues and doing research. When he was near Fort Valley, he would often spend the night with the Bonds. There were few hotels in the area, and most did not permit blacks to stay in them.

On March 14, 1942, Dr. and Mrs. Bond sat talking in their living room with Dr. Du Bois and Dr. E. Franklin Frazier, another well-known black scholar and sociologist. They discussed the events of the day, they touched on racial issues, and then the conversation turned to the subject of families and children. Somehow they came up with the idea of having a ceremony to welcome little Julian and his sister, Jane, into a life of scholarship. They wanted the children to understand the importance of learning.

Dr. Bond decided the occasion called for champagne. However, no alcohol was sold in Fort Valley. He drove into nearby Macon County and bought two bottles. When he got back, the three men donned the heavy black robes of college professors and called Julian and Jane into the room. Each of the men gave a little speech about the benefits of education, then signed a document on a nearby table. Mrs. Bond signed, too. The adults concluded the ceremony with sips of champagne.

Julian and Jane were uncertain about what had taken place. Mrs. Bond later said, "The poor children were scared to death."[4] Dr. Bond, however, had high hopes for the outcome of the induction ceremony. He said, "I wanted them all to become college professors."[5]

In 1945, when Julian was five years old, his father was offered the presidency of Lincoln University, a black college located near Oxford Township in Pennsylvania. Lincoln was much larger than Fort Valley State. Dr. Bond accepted the offer and moved his family to Pennsylvania. Julian's brother, James, was born that same year.

Julian enjoyed being on the Lincoln University campus. His family lived in the president's house, which was the biggest house on campus. They had

Julian and his sister, Jane, were not sure what was going on when three important African-American scholars—their dad, Horace Mann Bond, right; W. E. B. Du Bois, left; and E. Franklin Frazier—created a special ceremony honoring education for the children.

access to the school's gymnasium, tennis courts, and playing fields.

Julian Bond later said, "It was a wonderful place to grow up because of all the students around, all men at that time. It was like having four to five hundred big brothers."[6]

The only children who lived on campus were the

children of administrators and faculty members. Dr. J. Newton Hill, Lincoln's dean of students, and his family lived next door to the Bonds. The Hills had two daughters who were about Jane's age, and the three girls spent lots of time together. Dr. and Mrs. Lawrence Foster also lived nearby. They had an older daughter, as well as a son who was Julian's age. Julian and Larry Foster ran all over the campus, often accompanied by Julian's dog, Poppy. There were more children at Lincoln Village, but they lived too far away for Julian to play with them when school was not in session.

Mrs. Bond sometimes took her children to Nashville to visit family. These visits were very exciting to Julian because he got to ride on the train. "When we would go from Philadelphia to Nashville, we rode in sleeping cars," said Bond.[7] Sleeping cars had compartments, or berths, that folded down into beds. Julian liked climbing into the berths.

Julian never forgot one particular train ride. He and Jane and Mrs. Bond were hurrying through the train station when someone intruded. "I remember walking through the white section of the segregated Nashville train station and a policeman said something to my mother like, 'This is not for niggers!' My mother said very angrily, 'Don't call me a nigger!' and just strode by him with us following along. I don't think I was old enough to remember what this was really all about, but I do remember being impressed that my mother stood up to this authority figure."[8]

Most of Bond's memories of Nashville are pleasant. "My grandmother lived there with her second husband, the Reverend Brumfield. He was the chaplain at Fisk University, so it was like visiting another college campus.

"I had a godfather named Jean Price who was a pharmacist. He owned a drugstore right across the street from Fisk and he used to make fabulous chocolate sundaes for me."[9]

On Saturdays, Bond would see movies at the Nashville cinema. "I loved to see the serials, which they don't have anymore," he said. Serials were short, continuing stories shown in fifteen-minute segments. "You'd see one chapter of a story; it would be a cliffhanger where the hero was hanging from his fingernails to a railroad grid. You'd see the train approaching and the movie would end. When you came back the next week, he'd still be there, but he'd escape. By the end of the movie, he'd be tied down to the railroad tracks and the train would be coming. And on and on."[10] After the movies, Julian would go to Price's drugstore for a chocolate sundae.

When it was time for school, Julian did not attend a segregated school. "My sister and I integrated the schools of Lower Oxford Township, Pennsylvania," said Bond. "My father filed a lawsuit to get us admitted, but the suit never came to trial. They just caved in.

Many important people visited the Bond home. Here, Julian meets the famous singer and activist Paul Robeson.

There was a black school on one side of the street and a white school on the other side of the street. [The school board] just closed the black school and fired the teacher and all the kids just crossed the street."[11]

"I have no idea what happened to Mrs. Brown," said Bond, "but like so many black teachers, she was a casualty of the integration wars. . . . Mrs. Brown didn't lose her job because black people wanted to integrate the schools; Mrs. Brown lost her job because white people didn't want a black teacher teaching their children."[12]

The school bus stopped on the road behind their house, and the Bond children climbed aboard clutching their lunches. "We carried our lunches in tin lunch pails," said Bond, "not the kind kids have today named after cartoon characters. These were just standard workman-type lunch pails. We took a couple of sandwiches and a thermos filled with chocolate milk or juice."[13]

Julian and Jane did not always catch the bus home, though. "Sometimes we would hitch rides home with George, the driver of a bread company truck. George would let us sit in the back of the truck, and every now and then he would give us a sugar-coated doughnut," said Bond. "I have loved sugar-coated doughnuts ever since."[14]

Julian's early schooling was in a two-room schoolhouse. Two teachers were responsible for all the children. "There was one teacher in one room teaching several grades and another teacher in a room upstairs teaching several grades," said Bond. "I remember it was a big deal when you moved from downstairs to upstairs because it was like growing up in a way. Upstairs was where the big kids were, and all of a sudden you had become a big kid."[15]

Because it was a small school, the children got to know one another easily. At recess they chased one another and played baseball. They ate lunch outdoors when the weather was nice. Overall, school was enjoyable. The one drawback was the lack of plumbing. "The school had outdoor toilets," said Bond. "I didn't go to a school with an indoor toilet until I went to high school."[16]

In the sixth grade, the class was given an achievement test to measure reading skills. Julian got the highest score in the class. His mother said that getting the highest grade "just about ruined him."[17] Jokingly, she said that Julian had not opened a book since the test.

Julian's father was the first black president of Lincoln University. Sometimes the white administrators and faculty members had difficulty accepting a black man in this role. There was resentment against his authority.

The neighboring white community also had trouble accepting Dr. Bond. He was outspoken about segregation and other racial issues. He had sued the local school board and forced integration. His views and his activism sometimes caused others to act.

The Lincoln University students staged a sit-in at the Oxford, Pennsylvania, movie theater to protest the seating policy. Whites sat downstairs, but blacks had to sit upstairs in the balcony. At a sit-in, a group of people sit down somewhere to support or protest a cause. When asked to leave, they refuse. Sometimes the people are dragged away; sometimes they are arrested.

This was Julian's first encounter with a sit-in. He was too young to participate, and he was just beginning to understand what it was all about. The sit-in created tension in the community.

One night Julian and his family were out on their porch talking and enjoying the evening breeze. A car drove slowly by. The family continued to talk, not noticing that the car had stopped. Suddenly they heard several loud cracks. The Bonds jumped up, startled, then Dr. Bond hustled his family inside. "Someone had actually taken a couple of shots at our house," said Julian Bond.[18]

By the age of twelve, Julian had completed elementary school and was ready for high school. His parents thought about what would be best. They had already decided the local high school did not have much to offer. Jane had gone to the Cambridge School, a private boarding school near Boston, Massachusetts.

The Cambridge School had a good reputation. Dr. Bond's brother, Max, had sent his children there and they had done well. However, Jane was not happy at the school. She was one of only a few black students and she did not like it there. She begged to come home.[19]

While the Bond family wrestled with the decision of what to do about Julian's education, one of Dr. Bond's former students came to visit. James Streetz, a graduate of Lincoln University, was teaching at George School, a private Quaker prep school in Newtown, Pennsylvania. Streetz wanted the Bonds to consider George School for Julian.

Dr. Bond was hesitant. George School had come under scrutiny several years earlier when it had denied admission to a child of Ralph Bunche. Bunche, a well-known African American, was a representative to the United Nations at the time. Dr. Bond questioned Streetz about the Bunche decision.

Streetz explained that the school was now looking for qualified African-American students.

"I think he sold my father on the idea that it was a good school and that it would give me a superior education," said Bond. "The school wanted to have more black students than it did. I think my parents thought . . . the experience would be valuable to me."[20]

After much discussion, the Bond family agreed. Julian would attend George School in the fall of 1952.

3

SCHOOL DAYS

welve-year-old Julian was away from home for the first time and living in a school dormitory. "I was immensely lonely at first," said Bond. "I was the only black boarding student. There was another black day student at the school, but he was a senior and I hardly ever saw him. For a short period, I was really miserable."[1]

Julian's loneliness did not last long. He quickly made friends, starting with his roommate, Peter Steward. The boys decided who would get which bunk and how to decorate the small room they shared. They ate their meals in a large dining hall with other students at the school. When lights were turned off at 9:30, they whispered in the dark.

The students did not have to wear uniforms to school. However, the boys did have to wear a coat and tie to dinner and to meetings—the religious services held by the Quakers.

Bond said, "We had silent meetings every Sunday and Wednesday morning. There is no sermon, there is no singing. The meeting began when two men sitting in the front on a platform shook hands. Then, if someone was moved by the spirit to speak, that person stood up and spoke. If someone was moved to respond to that talk, he or she stood and talked. The Quaker meeting is a wonderful experience."[2]

Julian was naturally friendly and outgoing, so as time went by he made more friends and got involved with school activities. He also participated in a number of sports. He played goalie on the soccer team, swam backstroke on the swim team, and wrestled. The track coach tried to get him to run track, but that did not work out. Julian was not a runner.

"I think the coach of the track team believed all Negroes were superb athletes," said Bond. "He thought I'd make a great sprinter. I could barely run around the block, but he persisted in having me run up and down, up and down."[3]

When Julian's parents came to visit, they would ask him how things were going at the school. His mother, particularly, looked for signs of unhappiness. She looked to see how Julian and the other boys interacted. On one visit she observed Julian and two boys walking toward her. Julian had his arms around the boys as they walked up, laughing and talking. Mrs. Bond said, "Look Horace! He has his arms around *them*—they don't have their arms around him."[4] Still, Dr. and Mrs. Bond seemed satisfied that Julian had adjusted to the school.

Things were going well. Julian had settled in nicely and was having a good time. He was involved in a number of activities on campus and had lots of friends. People rarely said or did anything to make him uncomfortable, but it did happen occasionally. Bond later recalled incidents such as this one: "You'd be sitting around a room, and some kid gets a package from home and there'd be some cakes in it. He'd pass it around and miss somebody and that kid would say: 'What am I—a *nigger* or something?' . . . Then he'd say, 'Oops! Bond's here!'"[5]

As time passed, Julian was given the opportunity to live off campus in the home of a faculty member. This privilege was usually reserved for upperclassmen or for those students who excelled academically. Julian fit neither category, but he was offered the opportunity just the same. He and three friends—Peter Steward, Rafe Teller, and Claude Robinson—shared two rooms and a bathroom on the second floor of a teacher's home.

"This was much more pleasant than living in the dorm," said Bond.[6] There was much more freedom. One change that Julian particularly liked was that they could keep the lights on after 9:30. He could read late into the night if he wished. He often read adventure stories, especially those written by Arthur Ransome.

"Ransome wrote a series of books set in England in the Lake District about a group of children who are on holiday from school," recalled Bond. "They get into adventures pretending to be pirates, pretending to be Amazons, pretending all kinds of things—living a very rich fantasy life in which they had real adventures. Never life-threatening, but always exciting.

"I just pored over those books. The children's lives were very, very different from mine. Most of the books featured sailing. I'd never been sailing in my life and these were kids my age doing this. I identified very strongly with them."[7]

The boys were also allowed to play a radio,

In high school, Bond enjoyed school activities and sports, including soccer, swimming, and wrestling.

which had not been permitted in the dorm. Julian had a crystal radio set that he kept under his bed. Late at night he would tune in to some of the rhythm and blues stations in Philadelphia. He could also pick up *Randy's Record Hop* on WLAC out of Nashville, Tennessee. *Randy's Record Hop* was a program that played rhythm and blues as well as rock and roll. The radio signal was strongest late at night and could be picked up far across the country.

When Julian had time for television, he watched the *Colgate Comedy Hour*, *Your Show of Shows*, and movies starring Dean Martin and Jerry Lewis. "In 1956 or so, I began to watch the show *American Bandstand*. It was broadcast locally from Philadelphia for about a year before it became a national show and Dick Clark became the host," said Bond.[8]

"This was tremendously exciting because here were young people, a little older than I was, dancing on TV. There was usually always one black couple, boy and girl, so they could dance with each other," said Bond. "I guess so there would not have to be any interracial dancing. It was very exciting to see people your own age appearing on TV and to hear music that you knew was your music, teenage music, being played on TV."[9]

On Friday evenings, students from George School would often go into town to see a movie. One night when Julian and a group of friends were on their way back to school, they were assaulted by a bunch of town boys.

"There was kind of a gate that you walked through to get into the school grounds," said Bond. "There was a crowd of white kids standing there and they began to attack us."

There was a lot of pushing, shoving, and name-calling. A few George School kids were knocked down, but "nobody was hurt seriously," said Bond. "I guess these town kids resented us, thinking that we were rich, spoiled brats. . . . Probably, quite a lot of us were."[10]

As Julian grew older, he became interested in girls, but there were no black girls on campus. The only girls around were white, so he dated white girls. There were not many things to do or many places to go around George School. When the boys wanted to take girls out on a date, they went to town.

"What we would do when we went to town was go to the movies," recalls Bond, "or to an ice cream shop in town called Goodnoes." Goodnoes served ice cream, sundaes, and sodas. "The big deal was to go to town, sometimes on bicycle, but usually by walking, with your girlfriend on a Saturday afternoon and get some ice cream."[11]

One day Julian was called into the dean's office and berated for wearing his George School warm-up jacket into town. The warm-up jacket was black with white sleeves. GEORGE SCHOOL was boldly lettered across the back. When a boy got a jacket, he wore it on campus and he wore it to town. It was unreasonable that Julian should be scolded for doing something that most George School boys did.

"I believed that it was because I was going to town with my white girlfriend. The dean was disturbed because there had been a lot of clashes between boys from the town and boys from the school," explained Bond.[12] "He thought that identification of an inter-racial couple with the school might heighten some of the tension."[13]

Another disturbing event occurred to make Julian question the realities of life. Fourteen-year-old Emmett Till, from Chicago, had gone south to visit relatives. When he was accused of whistling at a white woman, two white men shot him and mutilated his body. Till's death made national news.

"I remember the death of Emmett Till in 1955," said Bond. "It impressed me because Till was fourteen and I was fifteen. Here's somebody my age being murdered because he stepped across the color line. I knew that black adults had been murdered in the past and I was frightened of those kinds of things, but they seemed kind of distant. But here was this fourteen-year-old kid getting killed and I was fifteen. I was terrified. I had to think if they would do that to him, what won't they do to me?"[14]

Julian's academic performance at George School

was not remarkable. He did just enough to get by. The teachers were puzzled because he was so inconsistent. One day his work would be outstanding. His teachers would get excited and praise him for his brilliance. A few days later the work turned in would be barely passing. They could not figure him out.

His grades reflected this behavior. Sometimes he made A's in his courses and sometimes he made C's and D's. Because of his up-and-down performance, Julian took five years to complete high school.

"I had to repeat my first year," said Bond. "Looking back on it—although it was a miserable thing to do because it meant that all the people I had gone to school with for one year had advanced and I was in the same place—I think it was probably the right thing to do."[15] Julian graduated from George School in 1957; he was seventeen years old.

Dr. Mordecai Johnson, president of Howard University, a black college located in Washington, D.C., gave the graduation speech. "I think part of the reason they invited him was because my father knew Dr. Johnson," said Bond. "Dr. Johnson was black and I was a black person graduating from the school. Also," he added, "Dr. Johnson was recognized as one of the premier orators of his day."[16] Johnson discussed the landmark school desegregation case *Brown* v. *Board of Education*. In that case the Supreme Court outlawed legalized segregation in the United States.[17]

Bond will never forget his days at George School. "They taught me lessons, which I didn't appreciate at the time, about nonviolence, about caring for other people, about service, about devoting at least a portion of your life to serving others. I absorbed that from the school and I am forever grateful to them. It was a wonderful, wonderful education."[18]

Bond was expected to go to college; his parents had emphasized the importance of education since he was a child. He applied to Lincoln University and Morehouse College, an all-male black college located in Atlanta, Georgia. Bond was accepted by both. While he wrestled with the decision of which school to attend, some things happened at home that helped him choose.

4

SITTING IN

r. Bond, Julian's father, got into a dispute with the trustees of Lincoln University. He was tired of the hassles and decided to leave the school. When Atlanta University offered him the position of dean of the school of education, Dr. Bond accepted. In the summer of 1957, the Bond family moved to Atlanta.

While driving around Atlanta, Dr. Bond pointed out what Julian thought was Morehouse College. Julian was smitten by the beautiful campus and immediately made his decision—Lincoln was out and Morehouse was in. Later, Julian discovered that what he had thought was Morehouse was actually Atlanta University.[1]

Julian lived at home while attending Morehouse College. He could easily get to his classes while living there and save money on expenses. He did not join a fraternity. Bond recalled, "When we lived in Lincoln, we had students living in our house. I can remember boys coming back from frat meetings with blood on the seats of their pants. I thought, 'Nobody's going to beat me so bad that I bleed and then call me a brother. No way.'"[2] Even though paddling was illegal, it was a common occurrence during fraternity initiations.

Julian's best friends at Morehouse were Leonard Hicks from Florence, Alabama, and Richard Hope from Nashville. They did the typical things young men do—they went to football games, parties, and dances. They also went to nightclubs and bars. "Atlanta had a very aggressive black nightlife with local singers and performers," said Bond.[3] The students enjoyed it.

Julian joined the swim team at Morehouse. The college had just built a new gym and put in an Olympic-size swimming pool. Julian swam backstroke and dived in high school, but at Morehouse he just swam backstroke. "We had a diver who had been an air force champion somewhere and he was fabulous," said Bond. "I couldn't compete with him."[4]

Morehouse was a member of the Southern Intercollegiate Athletic Conference. The team traveled

The Bond family in 1959: Julian, center, with James, Jane, and their parents.

all over the South, competing against other southern schools. "We'd get into sort of a big station wagon and drive to Talladega, Alabama. We'd swim against the local Talladega team and either spend the night or drive back. We were pretty good." said Bond. "Certainly not the greatest team in the conference, but pretty good."[5] Bond earned a letter in swimming.

Something else that carried over from his high school days was his love of writing, especially poetry. This gift was recognized by one of Julian's college professors, who helped him and others to showcase their talent in a literary magazine called *The Pegasus*.

"*The Pegasus* really was the inspiration of Dr. Esta Seton," said Bond. "She had a few of us who liked to write and she put together this magazine. I don't think it had more than one issue. . . . but it was quite an accomplishment for us to put this thing together."[6]

In 1958 Julian and three friends decided to go to Cuba. They drove to Miami, Florida, and spent the night with a college friend. The next morning they drove down to Key West and took a ferry to Cuba. The Cuban revolution had not yet taken place, and travel was unrestricted.

"We had a wonderful time," recalled Bond. "We went to the world-famous outdoor nightclub, the Tropicana, in Havana. We saw a fabulous show like you might have seen in Las Vegas in its heyday. There was a big line of about fifty to sixty dancing girls, and there were jugglers and singers. Of course, it was all in Spanish, which we barely understood. . . . We spent about five days in Havana and just had a wonderful time."[7]

In February 1960, something happened to change the focus of Julian Bond's life forever. "I was sitting in Yates and Milton Drug Store, a black-owned chain in Atlanta. It was across the street from the Morehouse and Clark college campuses," explained Bond. "It had a lunch counter and booths and students came in to kill time between classes.

Bond was sitting there, sipping a soft drink and reading, when he was interrupted. "This student, Lonnie King, came up to me and held up a newspaper, *The Atlanta Daily World*. The headline read, 'Greensboro Students Sit-In for Third Day.'"[8] The newspaper article described how students in Greensboro, North Carolina, had held a sit-in at a local Woolworth's five-and-dime store. These students, mostly from North Carolina A&T State University, had gone into Woolworth's and bought some things. Then they sat down at the whites-only lunch counter and waited to be served.

The waitresses refused to serve them; it was against store policy to allow blacks to eat at the lunch counter. The students refused to leave. After an hour, they got up and another group of students sat down. They got up in an hour and another group sat down. This nonviolent protest had been going on for three days.

In 1960 there were very few fast-food restaurants. Many stores had lunch counters, small areas where patrons could sit down and order coffee, soft drinks, and food. Most southern lunch counters would not serve black people. The North Carolina students had organized the sit-in to protest this racial segregation.

"Lonnie said to me, 'What do you think about this?' I said, 'I think it's great.' He said, 'Don't you think it ought to happen here?' I said, 'Oh, somebody's going to do this here.' He said, 'Don't you think we ought to make it happen here?'" Julian paused before answering, "Sure."

"He and I and a third student named Joseph Pierce went around Yates and Milton Drug Store and talked to students there. Then we talked to more and more of our fellow students, making sure we had somebody from Morehouse, Spelman, Clark, Morris Brown, Atlanta University, and the Interdenominational Theological Center. We pulled all these people together and the group got larger and larger.

"Before we actually did anything, news of what we were doing got to Dr. Rufus Clement. Dr. Clement was the president of Atlanta University and, in effect, was the president of the Atlanta University Center, even though the schools had only loose, informal relationships with one another.

"He called us in and said, 'I know what you're going to do. I've heard the campus gossip that you're going to sit in. But,' he said, 'you Atlanta students are special. I want you to do something special. Why don't you write something that explains what you're going to do and why you're going to do it?'"[9]

Julian and the other student leaders thought this over, then agreed. "Another student, Herschel Sullivan, and I wrote what we called 'An Appeal for Human Rights,'" said Bond. "It listed the grievances black Atlantans had against the segregation system in Atlanta.

"We borrowed liberally from a little pamphlet called *A Second Look at Atlanta* that had been issued a few months earlier by a group of black academics and intellectuals making the same critiques," said Bond, "but most of the language was our own. The appeal closed by saying, 'We have pledged our hearts and minds and bodies to eradicating these injustices.' We got it signed by the presidents of the student bodies of each of the schools."[10]

Dr. Clement persuaded a private source to donate money to publish the appeal. "The appeal appeared as a full-page ad in the morning *Atlanta Constitution*, the afternoon *Atlanta Journal*, and the black paper, *The Atlanta Daily World*," said Bond. It came out the first week of March and "caused a tremendous sensation."

"The governor of Georgia said this obviously was not written by students. It sounds as if it had been written in Moscow, if not in Peking. But the mayor of Atlanta, William B. Hartsfield, said, 'These are the legitimate aspirations of our own young people and young people around the world.'"[11]

The Atlanta students called themselves the Committee on Appeal for Human Rights (COAHR). They discussed where to hold the first sit-in. They had already decided that their first targets would be in Atlanta; Atlanta was where they lived and went to school. What they still needed to figure out was what locations in Atlanta to hit first.

Another concern was legal representation. Who would defend them if they went to jail? "We went to a lawyer and asked him to defend us," recalled Bond. "He told us the law was not clear about whether black people had a protected right to eat at private, whites-only lunch counters. We decided to go to places where the law, if not absolutely clear, was a little clearer."[12]

The Supreme Court had already ruled on two cases that involved integrating interstate commerce. So COAHR selected two bus stations—Greyhound and Trailways. Bus stations were part of interstate commerce, but the Supreme Court rulings on integrating these stations had not been followed. The students also selected the train station and several public cafeterias. The date was set and plans finalized.

"The beauty of the sit-in movement was that for the first time, people who were not lawyers, who weren't professional civil rights workers but ordinary everyday people, anybody who could sit down, could participate in a sit-in," explained Bond. "All you had to do was agree to participate in a certain level of nonviolence."[13]

Julian dressed up on the day of the sit-in. As he looked in the mirror and knotted his tie, he went over the day's plans. He shrugged into his sports coat and reminded himself what needed to be done and why.

He walked out of the house and into a slightly overcast Georgia spring day. The date was March 15, 1960.

"We went to the train station. We went to the public cafeterias in the city hall, a couple of cafeterias in the state capital, and a cafeteria in a federal office building," said Bond.[14] More than two hundred students participated, each going to an assigned site.

Julian's group went to a cafeteria in the basement of city hall. "I remember feeling nervous as we walked in," said Bond, "but I was in charge of the group. I couldn't have my nervousness communicated to my colleagues."[15]

Julian picked up a tray and made his requests. "The black women gave me my food and looked kind of frightened but glad at the same time. I came up to the cashier, a white woman, whom I later found out was the manager of the restaurant. She said in a nice voice, 'I'm awfully sorry, but this cafeteria is just for city hall employees.' I said, 'You have a big sign outside that says City Hall Cafeteria. The sign says the public is welcome.' She said, 'We don't mean it.' I said, 'We are going to stay until you serve us,' and she said, 'I'm going to call the police.'

"The policemen came and asked us to leave," said Bond. "We refused; they put us all under arrest and took us away . . . in a paddy wagon. They took us to jail, fingerprinted us, and locked us up."[16]

Seventy-seven excited but very frightened student

protesters were crowded into a large holding cell. "We were exhilarated because we knew we had joined hundreds of other young people who had already done this," said Bond. "We were joining a movement. And we were frightened because we were in jail. Most of us had never been arrested before, or if we had it was for speeding or something like that. It was scary."[17]

The jail was a grim place and it was occupied by other prisoners. They eyed the students warily, but they did not say much to them. The students eyed the other prisoners. "We kept looking at them, wondering, What are these people here for? What did they do? We knew they didn't sit in," said Bond.[18]

Because so many people had been arrested during the various demonstrations, the police took one person

from each group for a court hearing about the charges being brought against them. Julian was chosen from his group. Then bail was set for the demonstrators.

Bond and his college friends started a group called the Committee on Appeal for Human Rights. They planned a day of sit-ins to protest segregation in Atlanta.

□□

Julian's parents knew that he and his friends were planning something, but they did not know the details. His mother said, "When the sit-ins started, there was great consternation, and most people like us were opposed to it."[19] The parents were afraid of what might happen, afraid of the riots and the arrests that might follow.

Dr. Bond had been away on business when the Atlanta demonstration started. He came home to a weeping and frightened wife. "Julian got arrested," she sobbed.[20]

News of the sit-ins and the arrests had been on the radio; people were telephoning. Car after car drove past the Bond home. Mrs. Bond later recalled, "All the businessmen, anyone who had money, would go down and make bail for the students so they get could get out."[21]

"By this time the whole Atlanta community was in a hubbub because so many of us were getting arrested," said Bond. After spending six or seven hours in jail, bail was arranged and the student demonstrators were set free.

"We went immediately to Paschal's restaurant in Atlanta," said Bond. "They served us a big chicken dinner. Then a couple of guys and I went over to Spelman College so that girls could admire us and tell us what heroes we were."[22]

5

COMMUNICATIONS DIRECTOR

ne girl who admired Julian Bond was Alice Clopton. Julian and Alice met at one of the planning sessions for the March 15 sit-in. As they worked together on COAHR projects, Bond began to notice her. He asked her to go out with him and she accepted. Soon they were spending much of their free time together.

COAHR selected other targets after the March 15 demonstration. The first sit-in was successful and they wanted to broaden their efforts. The students considered restaurants, department stores, and movie theaters. One of the new targets was the A & P supermarkets.

"The A & P food stores only hired black people as bag boys," said Bond.[1] COAHR wanted A & P to hire blacks in other positions. There were two A & P stores in Atlanta on opposite sides of the city. Picket lines were set up at each site. Alice walked the picket line and carried signs for days.

Bond's leadership efforts changed as the group became more active. He was heavily involved in the communications aspect of the movement. He still assisted with planning demonstrations and determining where each group would go, but his biggest assets to the Atlanta Student Movement were his talents for writing and speaking.

Bond wrote press releases, position papers, and letters to attract attention to or get donations for the movement. The press releases and position papers told people outside Atlanta what was going on and what effect it was having. Bond made speeches to keep people thinking and talking about the movement.

By April of 1960, news of the Atlanta Student Movement had begun to garner national attention. One of the people to take notice was Dr. Martin Luther King, Jr.

"We got a letter from Martin Luther King and Ella Baker inviting us to join other students at a meeting of sit-in students at Shaw University in Raleigh, North Carolina," said Bond.[2]

Dr. King was president and Baker was the acting executive secretary of the Southern Christian Leadership Conference (SCLC). SCLC was founded in 1957 by Dr. King and other black leaders to protest discrimination and racial segregation in the United States.

Bond, Lonnie King, and several hundred students from all over the South gathered at Shaw University over the 1960 Easter break. As a result of this meeting, the Student Nonviolent Coordinating Committee (SNCC) was formed. SNCC opened an office in Atlanta. Because of the initials, SNCC was soon pronounced "snick."

Bond did not accept a leadership role in SNCC right away. He stayed busy with COAHR and the Atlanta Student Movement. SNCC leaders were just as happy *not* to have Bond, at first. They were afraid the Atlanta people, meaning Bond and Lonnie King, would take over the group.[3]

Meanwhile, Bond and others in COAHR were dissatisfied with the way local papers were reporting their news. They were particularly disgusted with the *Daily World*, Atlanta's black newspaper.

Bond said, "The A & P was a big advertiser with the *Daily World*. I think the A & P company put pressure on the *World*, and the *World*, which was a conservative paper to begin with, began to editorialize against our protest. We managed to get some black real estate men to take their ads out of the *Daily World* in protest, but they couldn't do that and succeed in business. They asked if we would help start another paper.

"We did," said Bond. They started a paper called the *Inquirer*. "Carl Holman, . . . a professor at Clark College, became the editor and I became one of the writers. I ghostwrote a column for Lonnie King . . . called 'Let Freedom Ring.'"[4]

Bond also wrote a sports column. He had fun describing the adventures of a mythical athlete who attended Sam Houston Institute of Technology. "I invented this fabulous athlete named Sam Bernard," he said. "Between the halves of a basketball game, he would go down to the swimming pool and swim for the swim team and break records.

"Either nobody ever read it or they never called me on it," said Bond. "It's funny because I knew then and know now *nothing* about sports. The black colleges would send us press releases about their athletic teams, so essentially I just rewrote them."[5]

Bond and his peers found that it was a lot easier talking about running a newspaper than actually doing it. A newspaper does not write itself; someone has to write the columns, features, and various articles that make up the paper. Newspapers need money. Much of the money used to operate newspapers comes from advertising. Businesses buy space in the newspaper to advertise their products. Someone has to solicit those ads. The young people worked long and hard to get the paper out.

Bond worked as hard as everyone else. He wrote editorials, he wrote advice columns, he went out and covered stories. "I used to go down to the police station," he said. "They had a desk as you came in, and over to one side there was a basket. All the day's police reports were in there. You could go through them and see if there were any interesting crimes."[6]

Bond found all sorts of news in the reports, some of it shocking. "There was a woman, obviously deranged, who had tried to dig a hole and put her children in and cover it up." The *Inquirer* was a half-size, tabloid-style newspaper. "I put in what we used to call a circus front page. That's a front page with nothing on it but big shouting headlines, and this headline was just fabulous. It was 'WOMAN TRIES TO BURY HER THREE TOTS ALIVE.'"[7]

Bond and the rest of the newspaper staff encountered numerous problems as they tried to keep the *Inquirer* going. Getting the paper printed was not easy. Some printers refused to print it, others would not print it the way the staff wanted it done. When this happened, Bond had to help with the printing.

Sometimes the *Inquirer* staff disagreed over how various issues should be presented. They wanted to stay true to the cause, but *what* was the truth? They could not always agree. Bond was usually the voice of reason. He would often persuade the others to take his point of view.

Lack of money was another major problem for the *Inquirer*. The staff had difficulty selling enough ads to finance the paper. Many of the business owners they approached were already paying for ad space in the *Daily World*. They had difficulty seeing the value of advertising in both papers. To raise money, the *Inquirer* staff sold shares in the newspaper. Bond's parents bought $100 in shares to help out.[8]

Alice Clopton helped, too. Since Bond spent so much time at the newspaper office, Clopton spent time there, too. She typed and answered the telephone. She helped with the page layout. She and Bond discussed articles. Whatever Clopton could do to help, she did.

Bond eventually became the managing editor of the *Inquirer*. He spent long hours at

Bond's biggest contribution to the Atlanta Student Movement was his talent as a writer and a speaker.

the office. His time was divided between running the newspaper, collecting and reporting news, managing the Atlanta Student Movement, and seeing Alice Clopton.

In January 1961 Bond officially joined the staff at SNCC. As communications director, he did all the writing for the organization, including the press releases. A press release is information given to the media about the beliefs, actions, or ideas of a group.

"I wrote the press releases, I typed them up on a mimeograph stencil, then I would take a couple of reams of paper and walk about six blocks into downtown Atlanta to the offices of the National Student Association," said Bond.[9] In the office, he would run off the copies. After cleaning up the mess from the mimeograph machine, he would walk back to the SNCC office. There, he would fold press releases and stuff, stamp, and address envelopes. Then he would take them to the post office for mailing. Bond also handled most of the dealings with the press. He spent so much time on all these activities, he had no time for school.

Bond had been cutting class excessively. The creativity and energy needed to put together a newspaper and organize demonstrations drained him. He had little time or energy to spend on schoolwork or to attend class. He was exhausted when he finally dropped into bed. One day a professor had stopped

Bond's friend Carl Holman to ask "how young Bond was doing."

"Why, he's doing fine," Holman replied.

"Hmm, glad to hear it," said the professor. "He hasn't been to my class in six weeks."[10]

It became clear that something would have to change. Bond's grades were seriously suffering.

"This activity just took more and more and more of my time," said Bond. "It was just so much. The movement seemed more enticing than school. School was something that I could always do. So—I dropped out of school."[11] It was the second semester of his senior year.

Bond's parents were very upset. They had had some doubt about Bond's involvement with the student movement all along. Now one of their worst fears had come true. Julian had dropped out of school without earning a college degree.

Later that same year, Julian Bond and Alice Clopton decided to get married at the office of the justice of the peace in nearby Dallas, Georgia. The first time they showed up for the ceremony, they had forgotten about the blood tests that are required to get a marriage license. The next time they went, they forgot to bring documents that verified their ages. The third time, on July 28, 1961, they made sure they had everything in order. They walked out of the courthouse as Mr. and Mrs. Horace Julian Bond.[12]

The Bonds picked Dallas, Georgia, as the site for the wedding because they did not want their parents to know they were getting married. The *Atlanta Daily World* reported weddings that took place in Atlanta's African-American community. It did not report on such events from Dallas, Georgia. "I'm not really sure why we decided to marry secretly," said Bond. "It just seemed like a good idea at the time."[13]

After the brief wedding, the couple went back to the SNCC office and announced that they had just gotten married. At first their friends did not believe them. There was laughing and teasing and, finally, congratulations.

At the end of the day, Julian went to his house and Alice went to hers. They lived apart for several months before breaking the news of their marriage to their parents. Then they moved in with Julian's family.[14]

6

"I'M JULIAN BOND"

ulian and Alice Bond lived with his parents for several months. Then they moved to a small house on Euharlee Street near Morehouse College. In the next two years they had two children. Phyllis Jane was born May 28, 1962, and Horace Mann III was born June 30, 1963.

Bond continued to carry out the business of communications director for SNCC. He was married, with a family to support, and SNCC paid him $85 a week. Then, in 1965, something happened to change the course of his life.

A lawsuit had been filed in the federal court against

the state of Georgia. This lawsuit forced Georgia to reapportion its general assembly. Previously, rural counties with fewer people had more representatives in the legislature than urban counties with more people. The new system was based on the "one person, one vote" concept. This change gave urban areas more representation and created new positions, or seats, in the Georgia House of Representatives. Bond said, "I found myself living in one of those brand-new reapportioned districts."[1]

Ben Brown, another civil rights activist and long-time friend of Bond's, was in the same situation. Brown lived in the district next to the one Bond lived in. Brown decided to run in the Democratic primary for the legislative seat in his district. He wanted to sit in the Georgia House of Representatives and vote on issues important to the people in his district.

"Bond, you ought to try this," suggested Brown.[2] SNCC people agreed. One of the activities that SNCC had been heavily involved with was voter registration. Now it was time for SNCC to give the people someone to vote for.

Bond was undecided. He and his wife discussed the possibilities of his holding a public office. He talked with friends. "Why should I run?" he asked.[3]

They reminded him of the things he had already done. They talked of how much work there still was to do and told him that he was the man to do it. "Run for the seat, Julian," they encouraged.

"Maybe I will," Bond replied hesitantly.[4]

Howard Creecy, a local black minister, had decided to run for the seat in the 136th District. This made Bond think more seriously about entering the race. Why should Creecy run? Bond knew about his own accomplishments in Atlanta, but he wasn't too sure about Creecy's.

"Okay . . . all right . . . ," decided Bond. "I'll run."[5]

Once Bond made up his mind to run for the vacant seat, he had to figure out how to go about it. One of his decisions was whether to run as a Democrat or a Republican.

"I'm not embarrassed to say that I didn't know whether I was a Republican or a Democrat at that time. The only political act I had committed was to vote for [Democrat] John F. Kennedy in the elections of 1960," said Bond. "I cast my first vote for president, for John F. Kennedy, when I was twenty years old. The voting age in every state except Georgia was twenty-one."[6]

Bond thought long and hard over which party to join. To help with his decision, he looked at who represented each party. "I didn't want to be in a party whose standard-bearer in the last election was Barry Goldwater. Goldwater had voted against the Civil Rights Act of 1964. On the other hand, the standard-bearer for the Democratic Party was President Lyndon

Johnson." Johnson had succeeded to the presidency after the assassination of President Kennedy. "Johnson was beginning to make a mark as a civil rights activist. I decided that was the party I wanted to be in."[7]

Bond discovered that a filing fee of $500 was required to officially enter the primary. He borrowed the money from his parents and had his name placed on the ballot.[8] Bond set up campaign headquarters in a wig shop in the heart of the 136th District and started campaigning.

"At this time, campaigning was very different from what it is today, " said Bond. "We're talking about a campaign where you don't use TV and you don't use radio. I spent all day every day for a month or more going around knocking on doors . . . and passing out leaflets."[9]

Bond spoke at rallies organized by local political groups. He quickly realized that he did not like rallies. "I was getting nowhere that way. I was making speeches to a lot of candidates, but not to many people."[10] He preferred talking directly to the public. He continued to canvass door-to-door. He introduced himself at barbershops, shook hands at bus stops, and visited churches.

"Sometimes I went to two or three churches on a Sunday morning, speaking to the congregation and passing out literature. This was an entirely personal campaign. We went to the people."[11]

Bond visited people in their homes. Atlanta's black community had a number of social and civic organizations. The meeting dates were usually listed in the *Daily World*. Bond scanned the newspaper for information about meetings. Then he made phone calls.

"Let's say I saw a little piece that said, 'The Chestnut Street Social and Savings Club will be meeting at the home of Mrs. Annie Jones on Sunday.' I'd call Mrs. Jones and ask if I could come by. She'd say yes and I'd go to the home. There'd be about six elderly women drinking tea and talking about this or that and I'd make a pitch. 'I'm Julian Bond and I'm running for the legislature.'"[12]

Staging house parties was another way Bond connected with the people. "It was common at the time for the Coca-Cola company to give free Coca-Colas . . . to candidates for public office," said Bond. "I would get someone on a block to agree to host a house party, then . . . pass out flyers asking people to come. . . . When they gathered, we'd serve Coca-Colas and I'd make a little speech. Then I'd say, 'If I get elected to the legislature, what do you want me to do?'"[13] Bond developed his platform from these informal conversations.

Bond's parents helped by hosting small gatherings at their home. They invited people over for coffee or drinks. Then they would introduce Julian. Bond's proud mother even stopped people on the street and

"We went to the people," said Bond, explaining how political campaigns were run in the 1960s. In a rare relaxed moment, Bond carries a huge bunch of collard greens, a vegetable popular in the South.

told them that her son was running for the legislature and needed their vote.

Bond also had the support of SNCC behind him. SNCC workers from Alabama, Mississippi, Arkansas, and southwest Georgia would come to Atlanta and offer to help. "These people would go out canvassing for me and with me," said Bond. "They would give me an afternoon or a day . . . knocking on doors and passing out literature."[14]

Even though SNCC was a big help in Bond's campaign for the Fulton County seat, there were occasional differences of opinion. "I remember big internal debates within the Student Nonviolent Coordinating Committee about whether I would be selling out if I wore a shirt and tie," said Bond.[15]

Blue jeans and overalls were the norm. The SNCC workers were trying to blend in and make the rural people with whom they worked feel comfortable. "I thought it proper to be more formal in this first attempt at running for office so I wore a shirt and tie."[16] Bond won the May fifth primary; he defeated Howard Creecy by a large margin and then went on to win the general election in November 1965. He was twenty-five years old.

A few weeks later, a SNCC worker named Samuel Younge stopped at a service station in Tuskegee, Alabama, and tried to enter the men's room. The station owner shot Younge in the back and killed him.

The reason? Younge had wanted to use a bathroom marked "Whites Only."[17]

"This guy was a navy veteran," said Bond. "He lost one kidney during a shipboard explosion, so he had to go to the bathroom more than most people. The irony of this guy, who had lost his kidney in the service to his country, being unable to go to this bathroom was just too much. A lot of antiwar sentiment that had been roiling around SNCC just bubbled to the surface."[18]

It surfaced in the form of an antiwar statement issued by SNCC and endorsed by Bond. In this statement, SNCC openly criticized the United States involvement in the Vietnam War. A press conference was held on Thursday, January 6, 1966, to release the statement. Bond was not there; he was attending a meeting at the YMCA. SNCC's leader, John Lewis, read the statement and then answered questions.

Later that day and the next, reporters telephoned Bond to ask about SNCC's antiwar statement. "Do you agree with this statement?" asked Ed Spivia, a local radio news reporter. He turned on his tape recorder and waited for Bond to answer.

Bond said yes. "I endorse it, first, because I like to think of myself as a pacifist and one who opposes that war and any other war, and [I am] anxious to encourage people not to participate in it for any reason that they choose. And secondly, I agree with this statement because of the reasons set forth in it—because I think

John Lewis, left, Julian Bond, and Andrew Young, right, were three young leaders gaining recognition for their civil rights activism.

it is sorta hypocritical for us to maintain that we are fighting for liberty in other places and we are not guaranteeing liberty to citizens inside the continental United States."[19]

SNCC's antiwar statement was news, but Bond's endorsement of it was even bigger news. Newspapers quickly released the story. Big, bold headlines read:

"DEFY DRAFT CALL, SNCC CHIEF URGES"

"SNCC LEADER AND LEGISLATOR BACK DRAFT CARD BURNINGS."[20]

Radio and television stations ran special news bulletins.

As people across Georgia unfolded their newspapers on Thursday evening or Friday morning, they were confronted with the glaring headlines. Those who tuned in to their local radio or television news channels were greeted with the same information. In some sectors of society, Bond's statement was applauded. However, there were a number of people who disagreed with his antiwar position. The more they heard, the angrier they became.

Lieutenant Governor Peter Zack Geer, Jr., said, "There is no way that Bond can take the oath of office as a member of the House to honestly uphold the Constitution of the United States and State of Georgia in view of his endorsement of SNCC's subversive policy statement."[21] He urged a fight to prevent Bond from being seated. Representatives Jones Lane and James "Sloppy" Floyd volunteered to lead the fight.

Lane and Floyd had been members of the Georgia House for a long time, so they knew many influential people. When they read the headlines and the news stories that followed, they agreed that something had to be done about Julian Bond. They wanted to charge Bond with disloyalty and kick him out of the legislature. They called other members of the House to support their position against Bond. They called the governor and talked to a few reporters. The swearing-in ceremony was just a few days away; they had to work fast.

Again, bold newspaper headlines confronted the people of Georgia. This time the headlines announced impending charges against Bond. His loyalty to the state of Georgia and the United States of America had been questioned.

Bond was unprepared for the furor over his endorsement of the SNCC statement. "It seemed to be a perfectly reasonable statement about the war. One that you could disagree with, but not as vehemently as they did. I was shocked."[22] Saturday afternoon, Bond discussed the problem with his family.

"Julian, they will never seat you," said his father.[23] Bond's brother-in-law, attorney Howard Moore, told him not to say anything else until they figured out a way to control the damage.

Late Saturday night, Bond, Moore, and a group of supporters met at the home of state senator Leroy Johnson. Johnson, an African American, had spoken with the governor and the lieutenant governor earlier that day. He thought that if Bond offered some sort of apology, indicated that his statements had been mis-understood, maybe they could keep him from being expelled.

Most of Bond's supporters agreed with Johnson. Modify the statement in some way. Try to appear apologetic. Just get the seat.

Bond was not pleased with this strategy. He did not want to apologize. He did not feel that he had done anything to apologize for. He believed that what he said was right, and according to the Constitution, he had a right to say what he thought.

All day Sunday Bond struggled with what to do and what to say. He met with his father in the morning and they mulled over the problem. Should he stand by his statements or should he recant? Should he modify it in some way? He scratched out a rough draft of what could be thought of as a compromise.

Bond met with supporters from SNCC and the Atlanta community Sunday afternoon. Still he was undecided. Sunday evening Bond ran into the Reverend Ralph Abernathy, Dr. Martin Luther King, Jr.'s right-hand man.

"What are you going to do?" asked Abernathy.

"I don't know, Reverend Abernathy—some people want me to give in and beg forgiveness and say I was wrong. . . . I don't know what I'll do," said Bond.

"Well, just do something you can live with," counseled Abernathy.[24]

After talking with Abernathy, Bond made up his mind. He would not take back his statement. He would not modify it. The United States Constitution granted him the right to say what he believed; members of the Georgia House of Representatives could not take that right away.

7

EXPELLED

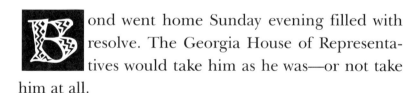ond went home Sunday evening filled with resolve. The Georgia House of Representatives would take him as he was—or not take him at all.

He thought of his constituents, the people who had voted him into office. How much did they understand about what was going on? They saw the headlines. They heard the news. What were they thinking now about their newly elected representative? Bond decided they needed to hear from him. He wrote a letter explaining his position and made enough copies for every person in his district. He wanted them to know exactly what was happening and why.

The next morning Bond prepared himself for the induction ceremony. As he dressed and sipped coffee, his mind was on the Georgia Statehouse. Would they take him? Would he be seated? Or would he be expelled?

Bond and his entourage arrived at the Georgia Statehouse a few minutes before the induction ceremony was scheduled to begin. News reporters shouted questions and photographers snapped pictures as Bond hurried inside. Reporters and photographers were even grouped around Bond's empty chair. As he took his seat, more pictures were taken.

At 10:00 A.M. on Monday, January 10, 1966, the House was called to order. People found their seats, organized their papers, and waited. The chaplain opened the meeting with a Bible reading and a prayer. Then the elections in each district were certified. The name of the person winning the seat in each district was entered into the books. Bond waited nervously while this was done. The next step was the oath of office. Maybe all this fuss would come to nothing.

Bond's hopes were dashed. "I will ask Representative-elect Julian Bond to stand aside. There have been several petitions filed to this office challenging his right to a seat," said the clerk.[1] Bond remained seated as his fellow representatives stood. He watched as they took the oath of office. They pledged allegiance to the state of Georgia and to the United

States of America. Then they denied any involvement with the Communist Party.

Bond had attended orientation sessions with some of these representatives. They had talked about the changes they would make and the good they would do once they were in office. Now the others would move on and he would not—not yet, anyway. Bond prepared for round two; he picked up his papers and stalked out.

He walked into a mob of reporters and photographers. They shouted questions at him. They asked how he felt about not being inducted. They asked if he was a Communist. Question after question was hurled at Bond. Camera lights flashed like crazy.

Bond tried to stay cool. He explained his position on the Vietnam War. He read from a statement he had prepared. He tried to be pleasant and polite, but they kept sniping at him. They kept asking if he was a Communist.

Finally Bond was fed up. "No," he snapped. "I am not a Communist. But I tell you now that I never intend to answer that question again."[2] He glared at the reporters. Then, after answering a few more questions, he sought privacy to speak with his attorneys. They needed to plan the next move.

George T. Smith, Speaker of the House, tried to get the opposing groups to compromise. He urged the group trying to unseat Bond to drop their petition; they would not. He tried to get Bond to modify his

Even though Bond had won the election, he was not allowed to take the oath of office at the Georgia Statehouse in 1966.

position; Bond refused. Left with no other options, Smith appointed a special committee of twenty-eight men to deal with the affair. Two of the newly inducted black representatives were assigned to this committee.

The committee was to hear arguments for and against Bond. Then it was to make a recommendation to the House. The full House would then vote to accept or reject the committee's recommendation.

The committee met in the House chamber. This way the full House, the people in the gallery, and the media could listen to the arguments. However, no one but the committee or the defense could speak at this time. Denmark Groover served as counsel, or attorney, for the petitioners. Howard Moore and Charles Morgan, a high-powered lawyer from the American Civil Liberties Union (ACLU), served as counsel for Bond.

Moore and Morgan used the argument that Bond had a right to say what he believed. Moore argued, "The issues here deal with Mr. Bond's right as a private citizen to endorse statements and express his views on the policies of the current administration. These proceedings aim to punish and harass him for exercising this right of free speech."[3] He and Morgan argued that Bond had broken no laws and was a patriotic and loyal American.

Bond was called upon to explain himself. Attorney Denmark Groover asked Bond whether he agreed with the SNCC antiwar statement. Bond said that he did. Groover asked if Bond approved of young men burning their draft cards.

Bond said, "I have never suggested or counseled or advocated that any one other person burn their draft card."[4] He had his own draft card in his pocket and offered to produce it. Groover did not ask to see it.

The taped phone conversation with the news

reporter Ed Spivia was introduced. Written transcripts of the tape were distributed to selected people. All were silent as the tape played. When the tape stopped, the Speaker asked if there were any more questions. There were none.

Bond's attorneys made one more attempt to persuade the committee to rule for Bond. They called four men to speak on Bond's behalf: state senators Horace Ward and Leroy Johnson; the Reverend Howard Creecy, whom Bond had beaten in the primary; and Malcolm Dean, whom Bond had defeated in the general election. They argued that Bond was young; this was his first political venture and he was bound to make mistakes.

The committee recommended that the House reject Bond. The House of Representatives was called to order again to vote on the committee's recommendation.

Prior to voting, members of the House were allowed to give speeches for or against the committee's recommendation. One after another, House members spoke, denouncing Bond. The Speaker of the House ended all arguments by calling for the vote. The House voted 184–12 against Bond. The resolution stated, "Bond shall not be allowed to take the oath of office . . . and . . . Representative-Elect Julian Bond shall not be seated as a member of the House of Representatives."[5] The meeting was adjourned.

Jones Lane and his supporters were jubilant. They had done what they set out to do—they had kept Bond from being seated in the Georgia House of Representatives.

Bond was stunned. "I didn't believe it. I didn't believe it would happen. I never thought—until the vote was taken—they would unseat me. I felt this terrible wrong had been done, to me personally, and to the people who had elected me."[6] He was also angry. "I had run for the office, I was qualified for the office, and I had won the office. For this group of men to tell me I couldn't sit in the office was just too much."[7]

Bond made his way through the crowd of reporters, well-wishers, and naysayers. He needed time to think and time to plan.

Bond took his battle to court. He charged the legislature with violating his constitutional rights to free speech, due process, and equal protection under the law. He explained his position to the numerous reporters who called or appeared on his doorstep.

Bond made national news. Newspapers, magazines, and television and radio stations across the country reported the unseating of Representative-elect Julian Bond. Major newspapers such as *The Washington Post* and *The Wall Street Journal* ran articles and editorials denouncing the Georgia House's actions. Dr. Martin Luther King, Jr., organized a march on the Georgia

Statehouse in support of Bond, and more than a thousand demonstrators participated.

People debated the Bond case in their homes, in coffee shops, and at work. Many agreed that Bond may have been foolish in saying what he did, but they supported his right to do so. The Georgia House was wrong not to allow him to take a seat to which he had been properly elected.

Others believed Bond was wrong to condone the burning of a draft card and that he was wrong about the war in Vietnam. Families with sons in Vietnam or veterans of other wars wrote to their state representatives condemning Bond. Meanwhile, his seat in the 136th District was declared vacant. A special election was called to fill the vacancy. Bond ran in the special election and won. The people of Atlanta voted him in—again.

Bond's lawsuit was argued in the federal district court on January 28, 1966. Three judges were selected to hear the arguments: Elbert P. Tuttle, Griffin B. Bell, and Lewis Morgan. Again, Bond's right to free speech was the primary defense.

Arguments went back and forth. On January 31, 1966, Bond lost in a split decision. The judges voted 2–1 that the House had the right to unseat Bond. When Bond's second winning of the 136th District seat came up for certification, the House voted again to bar him. This time, his opponents had the federal district court to back them.

Bond still would not give up. His seat was put on the ballot for a third time. Again, Bond won. Across the country, more people were rallying in his support. Congressmen sent telegrams to the governor of Georgia criticizing the House's actions. Hollywood stars made speeches on Bond's behalf. People took out newspaper ads supporting Bond and denouncing Georgia's House of Representatives. Ambassadors from fifteen black nations hosted a luncheon at the United Nations and invited Bond to speak. Popular opinion was growing in his favor.

Bond took his case to the United States Supreme Court. He hired two new lawyers, Leonard Boudin and Victor Rabinowitz, to file the appeal. His brother-in-law, Howard Moore, continued to work on the case, but Charles Morgan and the ACLU withdrew from it.

On November 10, 1966, Bond's case was heard before the Supreme Court. There, Georgia Attorney General Arthur Bolton argued that Bond did not support and uphold the U.S. Constitution and that he was not loyal to the government. The House believed that he lost his personal rights when he became an elected official. According to Bolton, the House of Representatives had the right to expel Bond.

Bond recalls, "I was sitting in the courtroom listening to the argument and I heard the attorney general

. . . make the argument that Georgia had the right to throw me out. Justice Byron White said to him, 'Is that all you have? You've come all this way and that's all you have?' I hunched [elbowed] my lawyer and said, 'We're winning, aren't we?' and he said, 'Yes! We are!'"[8]

Bond's attorneys argued that he *was* acting on behalf of his constituents. He was serving the people by making their needs and wishes known. He was entitled to disagree with the government.

On December 5, 1966, the Supreme Court voted unanimously in favor of Bond. The justices found that excluding Bond because of the things he said and opinions he endorsed violated his right to free speech. The Georgia House of Representatives *must* seat Bond.[9]

"When the Supreme Court overturned that decision," recalled Bond, "I was in Pittsburgh traveling someplace to make a speech. I was paged in the Pittsburgh airport, went to the phone, and it was a reporter from the Associated Press. He told me that the Supreme Court had ruled and that I was going to get my seat.

"I was overjoyed because the highest court in the land had said that the Georgia legislature was wrong. The three-judge federal court was wrong. Everybody who said I couldn't be in the legislature was wrong and I was right. And my constituents' . . . right to choose

Bond said he was "overjoyed" when the Supreme Court ruled that he could serve in the Georgia House of Representatives.

the person to represent them had been confirmed by the highest court in the land."[10]

On January 9, 1967, Bond finally took the oath of office. He had battled for this seat in three separate elections and won. He had pled his case in the federal district court and the Supreme Court. Now he savored the sweet taste of victory as he raised his hand and took the oath of office.

8

CHICAGO
1968

ometime prior to being sworn in at the Georgia House of Representatives, Bond resigned from SNCC. He no longer had time to fulfill his obligations to this organization. Traveling and making speeches kept him busy. He was also preparing to enter the legislature.

Another concern for Bond was that many of his SNCC associates were gone. They had graduated from college or moved away for one reason or another. Those remaining seemed to have a different philosophy. They still embraced nonviolence in theory, but they were beginning to encourage self-defense. Bond felt this was a mistake.

Bond's freshman year in the House of Representatives was not easy. "For almost the first year, most white legislators, including those from Atlanta and Fulton County, wouldn't even speak to me," said Bond. "In fact, my seat was the second from the aisle. White legislators would go by and talk to Ben Brown, who sat on the aisle. They'd ask, 'How's old Julian doing?' and Ben would turn and look at me sitting a foot away and say, 'He's doing okay.'"[1] "Well, you tell him to keep out of trouble," they'd say to Brown.[2]

"After time passed, these guys came to realize that I was a vote. I could be a vote in favor of their bill. I could be a vote against their bill. My vote may not have mattered much in the whole House, which was quite large; it mattered a great deal in committees, which were small. So they began to treat me like any other legislator."[3]

As a member of the House, Bond authored a bill to make low-interest loans available to low-income Georgians. Passage of this bill would make it possible for them to buy homes. Bond also initiated a sickle-cell anemia testing program. Sickle-cell anemia is a disease that primarily affects people of African and Mediterranean descent. It is a concern for African Americans.

"We [the legislature] had previously voted for a

Bond served on several committees at the Georgia Statehouse, where his desk was piled high with papers.

testing program for Tay-Sachs disease, a disease that is typically associated with Jews," said Bond. "Using this precedent of a testing program set up for a small portion of the population, I argued and won support for a sickle-cell anemia testing program."[4]

Bond came to national attention again when he was nominated for vice president at the 1968 Democratic National Convention in Chicago, Illinois. "In 1968 there was no popular election for the delegates to the Democratic National Convention the way there is now," said Bond. "Delegates were handpicked by the chairman of the Democratic Party."[5] Bond and a few others did not believe the delegation selected that year truly represented Georgia Democrats.

Bond's group, the Georgia Loyal National Delegation, challenged the delegation selected by the Georgia Democratic chairman. They organized conventions in each of the state's congressional districts and elected another set of delegates. Bond and the "challenge" delegates arrived in Chicago ready for a showdown.

Shortly after arriving in Chicago, they testified before the Democratic National Credentials Committee. The committee determined the number of votes for each state. After listening to Bond's group tell why it disagreed with seating the regular delegates, the committee decided to split the votes from Georgia. "There would be enough half votes so that all of the challenge delegates and all the regular delegates could be seated," said Bond.[6]

When the convention opened, all eyes were on Bond's group as the members sauntered over to the section of the convention center marked off for Georgia delegates. Word about the fight over the seating of Georgia's delegates had leaked out. The regular delegates were trying to fill the same seats. There was a little pushing and shoving and a lot of shouting as Bond informed the regular delegates of the credentials committee's decision to split the Georgia vote.

"Most of the regular delegates were so mad, they walked out and went home, allowing us to fill up almost all of their seats," said Bond.[7]

The Democratic National Convention went on. Hubert Humphrey received the presidential nomination, beating out Eugene McCarthy. There were still issues that other factions in the Democratic Party wanted to bring up, but they could not get to the microphone. To make a statement, a person had to be recognized by the chairman, then go to the main microphone to speak.

"You could raise your hand and shout and yell, but if you were a McCarthy delegate, you could not get recognized," said Bond.[8] Something had to be done to break the stranglehold that the anti-McCarthy Democrats had on the main microphone.

The ploy to get attention was simple: Nominate

someone for vice president. Whoever seconded the nomination could use the time to address the other issues. After much talking and political maneuvering, the group decided on Julian Bond. They explained to him what they wanted to do and why. Bond agreed and his name was entered as a candidate for vice president of the United States.[9]

Chants of "Julian Bond, Julian Bond" could be heard all over the convention center. From the convention floor to the rafters in the galleries, people chanted and screamed Bond's name. Those watching the televised convention from their homes marveled. Julian Bond was the first black man to be nominated for vice president. At twenty-eight, he was also the youngest. The U.S. Constitution required that anyone running for president or vice president be at least thirty-five years old.

A delegate from New York tried to get recognized to make the seconding speech. He was shouted down and the vote was called for. When Bond was polled, he used the time to decline the nomination. He said, "I deeply appreciate the honor, but unfortunately I have not yet reached the age and must therefore ask that my name be removed."[10] Bond received forty-eight and a half votes.

The 1968 Democratic National Convention was one of the most violent political conventions in U.S. history. There was a confrontation between antiwar

"I deeply appreciate the honor," said Bond at the Democratic National Convention in 1968. He was the first African American to be nominated for vice president of the United States, but at age twenty-eight he was too young to run.

students demonstrating outside the convention center and the Chicago police. What was supposed to be a peaceful demonstration turned into a riot. "The police lost control. They just beat the demonstrators senseless," said Bond.[11]

The students filled the intersection, shouting slogans and taunting the police. Suddenly, clouds of tear gas filled the sky. The police rushed the demonstrators, attacking them with nightsticks. Blows landed on heads, faces, and shoulders. Booted feet slammed into backsides, knocking demonstrators to the ground.

The students ran—coughing, screaming, crying—trying to escape. National Guardsmen in full riot gear toting rapid-fire weapons dragged students through the streets and threw them into police vans. Television news crews cut away from the convention floor to the madness taking place outside the convention center. In living rooms across America, people watched with horror. Finally the intersection was cleared. The antiwar demonstrators had been routed.[12]

"I was staying in the Hilton Hotel, right across from the park where the police beat most of the people," said Bond. "I remember coming back to my room and seeing bloody fingerprints on the wall. These people, who had been beaten in the street and come back to the hotel, obviously groggy and bloody, had touched the walls."[13]

Bond gave assistance to a young woman who had been slapped by a policeman. Kay Raftery had tried to enter the hotel. The officer had yelled "Stop," but Raftery did not realize he was talking to her until he had knocked her to the ground. When other police officers intervened, Raftery fled into the tear gas–filled lobby.

Julian Bond saw her trying to find the elevator. She was crying. Tears mixed with the blood on her face.

"Come on. I know a back way," said Bond.[14] He took her to the hotel kitchen and helped her clean her face. Then he showed her how to get upstairs using the service elevator.

"I very quickly discovered that service elevators were much easier to use than the regular elevators," said Bond.[15] The regular elevators stopped at every floor; service elevators did not.

The Democratic candidates did not win the election. People were unhappy with the violence at the Democratic National Convention, and opposition to the Vietnam War caused a shifting of allegiance. Republican candidate Richard Nixon was elected president, with Spiro Agnew as his vice president.

In 1971 Bond went back to Morehouse College to complete his education. "It was unfinished business,"

he said. He contacted student services at Morehouse to find out what he needed to do, and then he did it.

"I graduated from Morehouse College with the class of 1971," he said, "ten years behind the rest of my class."[16] Bond earned a bachelor of arts degree in English.

Bond continued to fulfill his obligations as a member of the Georgia House of Representatives. He sat on special committees, authored bills, and addressed the concerns of his constituents. He met other community obligations as well. He was a member of the Atlanta chapter of the National Association for the Advancement of Colored People (NAACP).

The NAACP was founded in 1909 in New York City by a group of blacks and whites who wanted to improve the plight of black people in the United States. The lynching of blacks was a common occurrence at the time. Schools were segregated—and those for black children were poorly equipped and offered a substandard education. Blacks were frequently denied all but the most menial jobs at very low wages. Public transportation and housing were segregated and inadequate. Blacks were not allowed to vote. The NAACP had made progress toward improving each of these situations, but there was still work to be done.

In 1940 a separate organization for legal defense was formed by attorney Thurgood Marshall. The NAACP Legal Defense Fund was necessary to shield the NAACP from lawsuits and legal harassment by hate groups. Years later, Marshall became the first African American to serve on the Supreme Court.

The NAACP was much more conservative than SNCC. Bond said he had joined SNCC "partly in protest because of the slowness and bureaucracy of the NAACP." Years later, "SNCC didn't exist anymore, but the old, slow, plodding NAACP was still there," said Bond.[17]

Bond was involved with the NAACP membership committee. He worked long and hard encouraging people to join the group. Often, when he had given a speech and was mingling with the crowd afterward, Bond would slip in a comment about membership in the NAACP. In 1973, he was elected president of the Atlanta branch office.

After serving seven years in the Georgia House of Representatives, Bond decided to run for the Georgia Senate. "My senator, Horace Ward, was appointed to a state judgeship by Governor Jimmy Carter. This meant his Senate seat was vacant," said Bond. "I decided to run for it . . . and I won."[18] Bond was admitted to the Georgia Senate in 1974.

The Georgia Senate is in session for forty days each year. Senators address budgetary issues, designate where state moneys will be spent, and conduct state business. They are assigned to various committees and work on committee business when the Senate is not in session. Bond served on consumer affairs,

In 1973, Bond was elected president of the Atlanta branch office of the NAACP.

government operations, human resources, and many other committees during his tenure as senator. One of his accomplishments as senator was to help establish a black medical school at Morehouse College.

By this time, Bond had five children to feed, clothe, and educate: Phyllis Jane; Horace Mann; Michael Julian, born in 1966; Jeffrey Alvin, born in 1968; and Julia Louise, born in 1969.

"Georgia legislators made $2,000 a year. I couldn't live off $2,000 a year by myself, let alone try to raise a

Wherever he went, Bond talked to people about racial problems and educational and economic differences. Here, Bond and John Lewis, second from left, talk with some field workers in 1975.

family," said Bond. "But I quickly discovered I could make money making speeches, so I spent an awful lot of time on the road traveling and speaking."[19]

Bond was very much in demand, particularly after being nominated for the vice presidency. Arriving home from Chicago in 1968, he had found himself bombarded with invitations to speak to all over the country Speeches became his main moneymaker. He spoke on a variety issues.

Bond earned up to $2,000 for each appearance, and he made about one hundred appearances a year. When the Senate was not in session, he traveled for speaking engagements or campaigned for fellow party members. As a result, he missed quite a few school programs and special events with his children. "I was away a good deal," he said, "but the good side of that was when I was home, I was home. I didn't have an office or a job to go to. I was home."[20]

9

THE VOICE OF BLACK AMERICA

ulian Bond's political career was going well. He was earning a good income on the lecture circuit. He was well known for his quick wit, intelligence, and smooth, melodious voice. In April 1977, Bond put these attributes to the test when he hosted the popular television show *Saturday Night Live*.

Bond flew into New York City on a Sunday to prepare for the show. He met with the cast each day to discuss topics for skits and jokes. As he got more comfortable with the cast and they got to know him better, the skits and jokes took shape. On Friday night they

In the mid-1970s, Bond's political career was going well, and he was in great demand as a public speaker.

ran through the program from beginning to end. Saturday evening, they held a dress rehearsal and a few minor adjustments were made.

"At 11:30 a voice called out, 'Live from New York, it's Saturday Night!' I came out and did a monologue, much of which I wrote myself," said Bond.[1] The show was a great success.

Bond did other televised projects. *Rush Toward Freedom* was his first narration. This performance was unique because it was an on-camera narration: The viewing audience could actually see Bond speaking. This was not always done with documentaries.

In *Rush Toward Freedom* actors reenacted important episodes in the civil rights movement—the student sit-ins, the arrest of Rosa Parks, and several other key events. The film was completed with someone else doing the narration at first. The producers viewed the film to see exactly how much time the narrator had to speak. Then Bond was brought in and placed in a recording booth.

"The producers would say, 'You've got to say this in ten seconds or fifteen seconds.' I'd repeat the line over and over until it fit exactly what the viewer was going to see on the screen," said Bond.[2]

Bond also used his public persona and voice to draw attention to the problem of world hunger by hosting *Global Paper: The Fight for Food*, a three-part documentary that aired on public television in 1978.

Julian Bond and his brother, James (in jacket and tie), visited with children at a community center in Atlanta.

Despite his busy schedule, Bond remained active with the NAACP. He had been president of the Atlanta chapter for several years, and in 1979 he was asked to apply for the leadership position on the national board of directors.

At the time, Bond was working on his first movie, *Greased Lightning*. The film told the story of Wendell Scott, the first black man to win a NASCAR race. Bond played the part of a reporter. The movie was being shot in Madison, Georgia, and Bond's contract specified that he could not travel more than forty miles from Madison during filming.

The NAACP committee interviewing the applicants for the national leadership post scheduled a meeting in Atlanta, which was sixty miles away. Bond could not travel that far; his contract would not permit it. He sent a message explaining that he could not attend the meeting. The message was never passed on and the interviewing committee selected another applicant.

The communication glitch kept Bond from being considered for the leadership position. "As far as they were concerned, I just didn't show up," said Bond. "I'm sorry it didn't work out."[3] Unfazed, Bond continued his work with the Atlanta branch.

Also in 1979, Bond provided weekly commentary on NBC's *Today Show*. He soon became recognized as one of the premier voices of black America. He spoke often and openly about racial issues. In 1980 he was selected to host *America's Black Forum*, a black-owned public affairs television program. This was an important assignment for him. *America's Black Forum* addressed a variety of racial, educational, and political issues. The syndicated program was carried on more than eighty-five stations across the country. Thousands of Americans tuned in each week to hear what Bond and his guests had to say. People became more familiar with his face and his voice. His importance as a political figure and civil rights activist grew.

The programs were taped in advance. Bond flew from Atlanta to Washington, D.C., every other week to tape the shows. When he finished one interview and that show was wrapped up, he taped another. He always prepared two or three shows at each visit. If something came up to prevent him from getting to Washington, there was always a prerecorded program to use.

Bond also wrote about the issues he discussed on *America's Black Forum*: racial discrimination, educational and economic disparities, voting rights, and the need for political reform. Articles carrying Bond's byline appeared in prominent national magazines and newspapers.

In September 1984, the Senate seat Bond easily won in 1976 was seriously threatened. Hildred Schumake, an Atlanta contractor, made a determined effort to oust Bond in the election for the 35th District Senate race. Schumake called Bond an absentee legislator and accused him of neglecting his legislative duties. Bond disputed the charges and defeated Schumake in the Atlanta primary by a very narrow margin.[4]

Bond began to receive awards for his dedication and community service. In 1984 he received the Legislative Service Award from the Georgia Municipal Association. In 1985 he received the Bill of Rights

Bond speaks openly about racial issues. He has become known as one of the top voices of black America.

Award given by Georgia's American Civil Liberties Union.

In 1986 Bond's smooth voice was heard on *Byline*, a radio program that was syndicated on more than two hundred stations. Bond discussed the same kinds of issues he addressed on *America's Black Forum*, but his time was limited to three or four minutes. He closed each segment saying, "This is Julian Bond for *Byline*."[5]

Bond's world began to shift in September 1986. He gave up his Georgia Senate seat to run for Congress. Four candidates vied for the congressional position in the Democratic primary on August 12, 1986. One of them was Bond's longtime friend and fellow activist John Lewis. Bond easily defeated all three candidates. However, he did not win by a clear majority. According to Democratic Party policy, in that situation a runoff election between the top two candidates must take place. That put Bond, with 47 percent of the vote, in head-to-head competition with John Lewis, who got 35 percent of the vote.[6]

The runoff election was scheduled for September 2. Bond was expected to win easily. Both men had campaigned aggressively. Each had a different approach. Bond, the son of college-educated, well-to-do parents, defined the meaning of style. He received endorsements from big-name political figures such as Senator Edward Kennedy and entertainment personalities such as Bill Cosby. He received the backing of most of the Atlanta city council members. He easily debated the issues, outtalking opponent John Lewis.

Lewis, the son of a sharecropper, heavily played up his workingman roots. Voters identified with his underdog status and working-class background. He was not as articulate as Bond and did not do as well in open debate.

Lewis began to attack Bond personally. One of the subjects that Lewis hammered Bond on was drug testing. Lewis had taken a urine test for drug use and passed it. During a radio debate, he challenged Bond openly, saying, "We can go outside and go to the men's room and take the test right now."[7]

Bond refused. He said such tests were unconstitutional and an invasion of privacy. He called the urine testing issue "Jar Wars."[8]

Allegations regarding campaign financing, paid endorsements, and misuse of city resources were flung about. Georgia politics had never witnessed such mudslinging between black politicians. Unfortunately for Bond, Lewis's tactics worked. Lewis defeated Bond by 3.6 percent of the vote.[9] Bond won the black vote, but Lewis won the white vote. People who had voted for other candidates during the primary switched to Lewis in the runoff election. The numbers were just high enough to edge Bond out.

After twenty years of public service, the forty-six-year-old Bond was out of office. In addition, his long friendship with John Lewis was over. "The most painful thing for me," said Bond, "was discovering that a man I've been friends with for twenty-five years didn't value the friendship as highly as I did."[10]

Things continued in a downward spiral. Bond's long absences and busy schedule had taken a toll on his personal life. Shortly after the election, he and his wife separated. For many, this was a shock. The Bonds had appeared to be an ideal couple, but the pressures of contemporary American life and the particular stresses involved with being married to a politician took their toll.

On March 18, 1987, Alice Bond got into a skirmish with a woman rumored to be Bond's girlfriend. The next day a furious Alice Bond went to the Atlanta police station and filed battery charges against the woman. While there, she accused her husband of cocaine use and suggested that his girlfriend was the supplier. She implicated several important Atlanta politicians in her accusations. The police launched an investigation.

Once again, Julian Bond made front-page news. He denied the charges. "I have never used cocaine, never at all."[11] Days later, Alice Bond withdrew her statement. However, a police investigation was already in progress, and the FBI was reviewing the case.

Black leaders spoke out against the investigation. To show support, black mayors recognized Bond for outstanding leadership and community service. In May they gave him the President's Award at the annual National Conference of Black Mayors in Miami, Florida.[12] In July the attorney general determined there was no hard evidence to support the allegations, and the investigations were halted.

All involved suffered significant emotional stress. Bond lost weight, smoked incessantly, and saw a skin condition worsen.[13] Alice Bond withdrew to the privacy of her home, leaning on family and friends for support. About a year later, in July 1988, Julian Bond filed for divorce. The divorce was final in September 1989.

10

CHAIRMAN OF THE BOARD

espite all the bad publicity, despite the intense scrutiny of his personal life, Bond was still a popular figure. After he narrated *Eyes on the Prize*, a video history of the civil rights movement, in 1987, and then *Eyes on the Prize II: America's Civil Rights Years, 1966–Present*, in 1990, Bond became even more popular. He was one of the top moneymakers on the speaking circuit. He narrated one or two important documentaries a year and continued to host *America's Black Forum*.

Bond had given up his Georgia Senate seat to run for Congress. When he lost the 1986 congressional

Julian Bond on a visit to the George School in the 1980s: At this school, says Bond, he learned important lifelong lessons about nonviolence and about caring for other people.

race, he was essentially unemployed. After much thought, Bond took his career in a new direction. In 1988 he began to teach the history he had lived.

"I got an invitation to teach at the University of Pennsylvania for a semester," said Bond. "I told a friend of mine who taught at Drexel that I'd be at Penn and said I hoped to see him while I was there. He asked if I'd like to teach at Drexel. I said sure."[1] By 1989, Bond was teaching at both Drexel and at the University of Pennsylvania.

"Fortunately, these schools were literally across the street from each other. It was easy to take the train from D.C. to Philly, teach at Drexel, eat dinner, teach at Penn, then take the train back home," said Bond.[2] He taught the History of the Civil Rights Movement, Southern Black Politics, and the Black and White '60s.

Bond's reputation as an educator grew, and he was asked to teach at Harvard University in Cambridge, Massachusetts. Then the University of Virginia, in Charlottesville, asked him to come in the fall of 1990. He eventually accepted a full-time position as professor of history at the University of Virginia, but he continued to accept invitations to serve as visiting professor at other schools.

Life was hectic trying to keep all the schedules straight. "Monday nights I'd drive a few blocks from my home to American University and teach one class there. Early Tuesday morning, I'd drive two and a half hours to Charlottesville, Virginia, and teach two classes Tuesday afternoon. I'd have office hours all day Wednesday, teach one class on Thursday afternoon, then late Thursday night drive back to Washington, D.C."[3] Every now and then, Bond would have to remind himself where he was and which class he was teaching.

However, he did find time to get married. On March 17, 1990, two months after his fiftieth birthday, Bond married attorney Pamela Sue Horowitz.

Dr. Bond's hopes for his son's academic life had come true. Julian Bond was a college professor, teaching at some very prestigious universities. He also continued to write professionally. He started a newspaper column, *Viewpoint*, which achieved national syndication. He had several papers and articles published: "Developing New Approaches to Civil Rights for the 1990's" appeared in the *Harvard Civil Rights/Civil Liberties Law Review* in 1990; and "Voting Rights: A Beneficiary's Perspective" appeared in *The American University Law Review* in 1994.

Bond enjoys teaching and hopes to encourage an appreciation of black history in today's youth.[4] "I tell my students that the [civil rights] movement didn't begin in 1900; it began when the first African slaves set foot on this soil. And it didn't end in 1964 or 1965, when the civil rights and voting rights acts were passed, or in 1968, when Martin Luther King, Jr., was killed. It continues today with different personalities and under a different guise, and it will continue . . . for many years in the future," said Bond.[5]

Over the years that Bond has maintained his association with the NAACP, his role within the organization has changed. He started out as a member and then became president of the Atlanta branch. Eventually, he was elected to serve on the national board of directors.

Bond served four terms on the sixty-four-member

Bond teaches the history he lived: "I tell my students that the civil rights movement began when the first African slaves set foot on this soil. . . . And it continues today."

national board of directors before being elected chairman of the board in February 1998. Once again, Bond made national news. He had become the head of the oldest and the largest civil rights organization. What were his plans? What was he going to do? How were things going to change?

"We're not going to do any new things, we're going to do the old things better," said Bond. "What do we do? We organize, we agitate, we litigate, and we form coalitions. Those are the four things that we do. And we do them in order to fight white supremacy."[6]

The chairman of the board is not a paid position. Bond receives no salary. However, expenses incurred while carrying out his duties are covered. Bond is not responsible for the day-to-day operations of the organization. That is the responsibility of the president. "I am the head of the policy-making arm of the NAACP," said Bond.[7] Policies are rules that guide the organization. Bond helps to determine what those rules will be. The chairman of the board of directors is elected for a one-year term, but can be reelected for additional terms.

The NAACP has more than six hundred thousand members and sixteen hundred branch offices across the United States. There are three hundred youth groups. The organization has more than $10 million in its annual budget, with a full-time staff of hundreds. The popularity and prestige of the NAACP waned in the early 1990s when the organization was rocked by scandal and discovered to be several million dollars in debt. Young people viewed the NAACP as old-fashioned. People had become complacent.

Bond worked to change that, helping to elect new NAACP leaders: a new chairman of the board, Myrlie Evers-Williams, in 1995; and a new president of the organization, Kweisi Mfume, in 1996. Through their efforts, the NAACP again became financially sound; it is no longer millions of dollars in debt. Bond is working on building the membership and attracting more young people.

As chairman of the board of directors of the NAACP, Bond continues the work he started with SNCC. Back then, in Atlanta, he led thousands. Today, from his home in Washington, D.C., and the NAACP national office in Baltimore, Maryland, Bond leads hundreds of thousands. He and John Lewis worked closely together in Atlanta until their friendship shattered during the 1986 congressional race. In Washington, D.C., Bond and Congressman Lewis share a common purpose and common goals: Both are fighting for social change and justice. Their relationship is amicable. They work together as needed to get the job done; they are not friends.

Bond believes he can help the NAACP achieve its goals with better technology. "I want to bring us up to the twentieth century," said Bond in 1998. "Quite often, the NAACP office in a town will be a telephone answering machine in somebody's living room."[8] He has also said, "I want to move us into the fax world, I want to move us into the e-mail world so that at the push of a button or the click of a pointer, we'll be able to mobilize this enormous constituency that we have."[9]

Bond has restored visibility and power to the NAACP. He wants the NAACP to be a factor in every decision in regard to race. "Wherever race is discussed in America, in the Oval Office, in the CEO's office, in the state capitol, in the city hall or in the corner barber shop, I want the NAACP's voice to be heard."[10] "I want people to be able to say, 'This is what the NAACP thinks,' whenever policies dealing with race are offered."[11]

Bond makes the board's position on various topics known by issuing press releases. "Typically, at a board meeting, we'd pass resolutions about the civil rights issue of the day, but we'd never tell anyone. . . . I've instituted a policy of announcing our resolutions at the end of our meetings. No longer will people say, 'What do you do? What are you for? What are you against?'"[12] By reading the press releases, people will know.

Bond and the NAACP have identified several priorities: achieving equality of education for all children at local, state, and federal levels; banning assault weapons and handguns; preserving affirmative action; eliminating racial profiling and police brutality; and eliminating unfair restrictions in the home finance and insurance industry. They are also targeting health issues such as AIDS, hypertension, cancer, and teen pregnancy in African-American communities.

The NAACP Voter Empowerment 2000 Campaign was another priority. "We need to dedicate . . . most of our energies . . . making sure every eligible black person is registered to vote, and that every registered black person turns out to vote," said Bond. "I want us to have a big impact on . . . elections."[13]

Julian Bond on a visit to the Weisser Park Community Center in Fort Wayne, Indiana, in March 2000.

Bond is particularly concerned about voter apathy, especially among young people. Today's young people do not remember the struggle it took to get African-Americans the right to vote. They take voting for granted. Many do not exercise the right their parents and grandparents worked hard to secure. Bond also wants to reverse some of the setbacks to affirmative action. To do that, everyone must get involved, everyone must vote.

Affirmative action is a government-sponsored program that encourages special consideration for minorities and women in educational, employment, and business opportunities. For example, if two equally qualified people were competing for the same position, the minority candidate would get the job.

Affirmative action programs were developed to make up for racial and gender discrimination that for years favored the white majority. Some people believe that these programs are not enough and that more needs to be done to ensure that minorities are fairly represented in universities and the workplace. Others believe that affirmative action is actually discrimination in reverse, and that it is not fair to whites. A lawsuit against affirmative action was filed in Michigan. California repealed its affirmative action program in 1998. Other states are considering making changes in their affirmative action programs.

In November 2000, the American people elected the entire House of Representatives, a third of the Senate, the president, and the vice president. The close presidential election was decided by only a few votes.

In coming years, other elections and other issues affecting civil rights may take center stage. However, Bond truly believes that discrimination and racism are handled most effectively at the polls. "The ballot box is the front line in the battle for justice and equality," said Bond.[14] He will continue to fight, continue to push, continue to encourage people to choose their destiny and vote.

11

RACE MAN

Julian Bond is taking life a little easier now. Instead of giving a hundred speeches a year, he makes about fifty. If the distance is reasonable, he avoids the airport and takes a leisurely drive. Unless he absolutely has to go out, he prefers to stay home. "If I never went out, it would be fine with me," he said.[1]

Bond likes to spend his evenings at home surrounded by the people and the things he loves. His home is filled with collectibles—antiques, paintings, figurines, and other forms of black memorabilia. His library shelves are crowded with books. Whether he is sprawled on the sofa or tucked away in his home office, the soft, sensual sounds of jazz fill the room. He has a large collection of tapes and CDs. His favorite artists include old jazz greats and songsters such as Billy Eckstine, Billie Holiday, Charlie Parker, Ray Charles, and Dinah Washington.

Bond reads a number of newspapers and magazines. When he picks up a book, it's generally a history book. He tends to read about race relations and civil rights history. When he's truly reading to relax, he may choose a mystery novel.

"I like to read what are called police procedurals," said Bond. "These are mysteries, generally British, in which the main hero or heroine is a police detective. The basis of the story is the reader learning how the crime is detected, how the guilty party is uncovered. It's really the skill of the policemen in tracking down who actually did it that is so fascinating."[2]

Another activity Bond really enjoys is letter writing, and he likes to do it the old-fashioned way. "I've always been a big letter writer," said Bond. "Even today, when we have the Internet and . . . e-mail, I still write letters. I even write letters to people here in Washington, D.C., that I can call up and talk to on the phone.

"I think there's something intimate and personal about a letter written on good paper with a real ink pen," Bond said, adding, "I'm not talking about a ballpoint pen but a *real* ink pen. And if someone writes me a letter, in ink, then I feel more attached to the message, whatever it is, than I do to an e-mail message or a typed letter or one written with a ballpoint pen."[3]

When asked about areas of excellence, Bond says communication is his thing. "I am excellent in formulating my thoughts and putting them into words, either verbally or on paper, in ways that should make it absolutely clear to everybody who hears or reads them exactly what it is I mean. I am very proud of my ability to do that."[4]

In 1987 Bond left office after an unsuccessful congressional bid. He had been elected to public office more than any other black Georgian. He had served four terms in the Georgia House of Representatives and six terms in the Georgia Senate. He had authored more than sixty bills that became law.

When Bond entered the private sector, he did not cease to serve. He has continued his efforts to improve the human condition through his work with the NAACP. He has served through his membership on a variety of boards and advisory committees such as the National Sharecroppers Fund, the Division of Preservation and Research for the National Endowment for the Humanities, and the *American Heritage Book of English Usage*. There are many, many more.

Critics say Bond has not lived up to others' expectations of him. To these people, Bond says, "I've done

Julian Bond, pictured here with author Denise M. Jordan, will never stop fighting for his goal: to end racial injustice.

the best I could with what I had."[5] Others look up to him with gratitude for what he has done. He is stopped on the street and asked for his autograph. People ask to be photographed with him so they can show family members that they actually met Julian Bond. "If people remember me, I hope it's not for what I've already done but what I'm still going to do," he says.[6]

His legacy to America's children will be one of service and activism. When invited back to speak at George School, Bond told students, "I hope that . . . a portion of your life and time is spent in helping others help themselves, in enlarging opportunities, in delivering hope."[7]

Bond lives that message. "It's not common now, but sixty to seventy-five years ago, there were figures in black America . . . who were thought of as race men. Men who had dedicated their lives to improving conditions for the black race," said Bond. "I want to be remembered as somebody who's spent most of his energies doing that. I want to be thought of as someone who fought for the race."[8]

CHRONOLOGY

1940—Horace Julian Bond is born January 14, 1940, in Nashville, Tennessee.

1945—Father accepts position at Lincoln University; family moves to Pennsylvania.

1952—Starts high school at George School in Newtown, Pennsylvania.

1957—Graduates from George School, enters Morehouse College.

1958—Takes trip to Cuba.

1960—Founds COAHR; start of Atlanta sit-in movement.

1961—Becomes communications director for SNCC; drops out of college, marries Alice Clopton.

1965—Is elected to Georgia House of Representatives.

1966—Endorses SNCC antiwar statement; is expelled from the Georgia House of Representatives; Supreme Court decision overturns expulsion.

1967—Is seated in the Georgia House of Representatives.

1968—At Democratic National Convention in Chicago, cochairs Georgia Loyal National Delegation and is nominated for the vice presidency.

1971—Earns bachelor of arts degree from Morehouse College.

1973—Becomes president of the Atlanta chapter of the NAACP.

1974—Is admitted to the Georgia Senate.

1977—Hosts *Saturday Night Live*.

1978—Narrates *Global Paper: The Fight for Food*.

1979—Provides weekly commentary on NBC-TV's *Today Show*.

1980—Begins hosting *America's Black Forum*.

1984—Receives Legislative Service Award.

1985—Receives Bill of Rights Award.

1986—Loses congressional race to John Lewis; marriage breaks up.

1987—Narrates *Eyes on the Prize*.

1988—Begins teaching career.

1989—Narrates life of Adam Clayton Powell, Jr.; is named a Pappas Fellow; teaches at the University of Pennsylvania; becomes visiting professor at Harvard.

1990—Narrates *Eyes on the Prize II*; becomes professor of history at the University of Virginia in Charlottesville; marries Pamela Sue Horowitz.

1991—Is named Distinguished Professor in Residence at American University in Washington, D.C.

1992—Is named visiting Professor of Political Science at Williams College in Williamstown, Massachusetts.

1998—Is elected chairman of the national board of directors of the NAACP.

CHAPTER NOTES

Chapter 1. "The Infamous Mr. Bond"

1. Marshall Frady, "The Infamous Mr. Bond," *Saturday Evening Post*, May 6, 1967, p. 94.

2. Advertisement in *The New York Times*, January 20, 1966, p. 23.

Chapter 2. Growing Up

1. George Metcalf, *Up From Within: Today's New Black Leaders* (New York: McGraw-Hill Book Company, 1971), p. 150.

2. Roger M. Williams, *The Bonds: An American Family* (New York: Atheneum, 1972), p. 185.

3. Richard Bruner, *Black Politicians* (New York: David McKay Company, Inc., 1971), p. 4.

4. Lee May, "Window on History: Julia Bond Views a Remarkable Past Through the Prism of a Long Life Rich in Notable People," *The Atlanta Journal-Constitution*, August 6, 1996, p. M-03.

5. Williams, p. 185.

6. Taped author interview with Julian Bond, February 2000.

7. Ibid.

8. Ibid.

9. Ibid.

10. Ibid.

11. C. Stone Brown, "Julian Bond: Leading the Movement into the Millennium," *The New Crisis*, January/February 2000, p. 28.

12. Taped author interview with Julian Bond, February 2000.

13. Ibid.

14. Ibid.

15. Ibid.

16. Ibid.

17. Williams, p. 184.

18. Taped author interview with Julian Bond, February 2000.

19. Williams, p. 186.

20. Taped author interview with Julian Bond, February 2000.

Chapter 3. School Days

1. Taped author interview with Julian Bond, February 2000.

2. Ibid.

3. Richard Bruner, *Black Politicians* (New York: David McKay Company, Inc., 1971), p. 5.

4. John Neary, *Julian Bond: Black Rebel* (New York: William Morrow and Company, Inc., 1971), p. 43.

5. Ibid., p. 43.

6. Taped author interview with Julian Bond, February 2000.

7–12. Ibid.

13. Bruner, p. 5.

14. Taped author interview with Julian Bond, February 2000.

15. Ibid.

16. Ibid.

17. Jack Greenberg, *Crusaders in the Courts* (New York: Basic Books, 1994), p. 116.

18. Taped author interview with Julian Bond, February 2000.

Chapter 4. Sitting In

1–18. Taped author interview with Julian Bond, February 2000.

19. John Neary, *Julian Bond: Black Rebel* (New York: William Morrow and Company, Inc., 1971), p. 55.

20. Ibid., p. 56.

21. Lee May, "Window on History: Julia Bond Views a Remarkable Past Through the Prism of a Long Life Rich in Notable People," *The Atlanta Journal-Constitution*, August 6, 1995, p. M-03.

22. Taped author interview with Julian Bond, February 2000.

Chapter 5. Communications Director

1. Taped author interview with Julian Bond, February 2000.

2. Ibid.

3. Roger M. Williams, *The Bonds: An American Family* (New York: Atheneum, 1972), p. 211.

4. Taped author interview with Julian Bond, February 2000.

5. Ibid.

6. Ibid.

7. Ibid.

8. Williams, p. 208.

9. Taped author interview with Julian Bond, February 2000.

10. Williams, p. 208.

11. Taped author interview with Julian Bond, February 2000.

12. John Neary, *Julian Bond: Black Rebel* (New York: William Morrow and Company, Inc., 1971), p. 63.

13. Taped author interview with Julian Bond, February 2000.

14. Neary, p. 63.

Chapter 6. "I'm Julian Bond"

1. Taped author interview with Julian Bond, February 2000.

2. Ibid.

3. John Neary, *Julian Bond: Black Rebel* (New York: William Morrow and Company, Inc., 1971), p. 75.

4. Taped author interview with Julian Bond, February 2000.

5. Neary, p. 77.

6. Taped author interview with Julian Bond, December 1999.

7. Ibid.

8. Taped author interview with Julian Bond, February 2000.

9. Taped author interview with Julian Bond, December 1999.

10. Neary, p. 79.

11. Taped author interview with Julian Bond, December 1999.

12. Taped author interview with Julian Bond, February 2000.

13. Taped author interview with Julian Bond, December 1999.

14. Ibid.

15. Ibid.

16. Ibid.

17. Taped author interview with Julian Bond, February 2000.

18. Ibid.

19. *United States Reports*, vol. 385, October Term, 1966, *Bond* v. *Floyd*, p. 121.

20. Neary, p. 102.

21. Roy Reed, "Georgians Score a Vietnam Critic: Negro Elected to Legislature Faces Expulsion Move," *The New York Times*, January 8, 1966, p. 3.

22. Taped author interview with Julian Bond, August 2000.

23. Neary, p. 102.

24. Ibid., pp. 106–107.

Chapter 7. Expelled

1. Roger M. Williams, *The Bonds: An American Family* (New York: Atheneum, 1972), p. 226.

2. Ibid., p. 227.

3. Ibid.

4. *United States Reports*, vol. 385, October Term, 1966, *Bond* v. *Floyd*, p. 124.

5. Ibid., p. 125.

6. John Neary, *Julian Bond: Black Rebel* (New York: William Morrow and Company, Inc., 1971), p. 124.

7. Taped author interview with Julian Bond, December 1999.

8. Taped author interview with Julian Bond, February 2000.

9. *United States Report*, Volume 385, October Term, 1966, *Bond* v. *Floyd*, p. 137.

10. Taped author interview with Julian Bond, December 1999.

Chapter 8. Chicago 1968

1. Taped author interview with Julian Bond, February 2000.

2. George Metcalf, *Up From Within: Today's New Black Leaders* (New York: McGraw-Hill Book Company, 1971), p. 175.

3. Taped author interview with Julian Bond, February 2000.

4. Taped author interview with Julian Bond, December 1999.

5. Ibid.

6. Ibid.

7. Ibid.

8. Ibid.

9. Ibid.

10. Emily Rovetch, *Like It Is: Arthur E. Thomas Interviews Leaders on Black America* (New York: E. P. Dutton, 1981), p. 145.

11. Taped author interview with Julian Bond, February 2000.

12. "Chicago 1968," *The American Experience*, produced by Chana Gazit, distributed by PBS Video, 1995, WGBH, Boston, Massachusetts.

13. Taped author interview with Julian Bond, August 2000.

14. Kay Raftery, "It Was 1968, and Julian Bond Rescued Me," *The New York Times*, August 28, 1993, pp. 15, 19.

15. Taped author interview with Julian Bond, August 2000.

16. Taped author interview with Julian Bond, February 2000.

17. Ibid.

18. Ibid.

19. Ibid.

20. Ibid.

Chapter 9. The Voice of Black America

1. Taped author interview with Julian Bond, August 2000.

2. Ibid.

3. Ibid.

4. "Bond Holds Off Foe in Georgia State Senate Race," *Jet*, September 3, 1984, p. 24.

5. Taped author interview with Julian Bond, August 2000.

6. Ann Kimbrough, "The Fight for the Fifth," *Black Enterprise*, November 1986, p. 21.

7. "Lewis Victory Strains His Long Friendship With Bond," *Jet*, September 22, 1986, p. 4.

8. Ron Taylor, "Old Comrade Beats Bond by 3.6% of Vote," *The Atlanta Journal-Constitution*, September 3, 1986, p. A-01.

9. Ibid., p. A-01.

10. Priscilla Painton, "Bond Keeps His Cool, Retains Popularity in Midst of Crisis," *The Atlanta Journal-Constitution*, May 17, 1987, p. A-01.

11. William E. Schmidt, "Bond Denies Wife's Initial Story and Says He Never Used Cocaine," *The New York Times*, April 15, 1987, p. A16.

12. "Julian Bond Given Black Mayors' Award," Jet, May 11, 1986, p. 7.

13. Painton, p. A-01.

Chapter 10. Chairman of the Board

1. Taped author interview with Julian Bond, August 2000.

2. Ibid.

3. Ibid.

4. Kevin Chappell, "Where Are the Civil Rights Icons of the '60's?" *Ebony*, August 1996, p. 108.

5. Douglas Brinkley, "Places at the Heart of the Movement," *American Legacy*, Summer 1997, p. 12.

6. C. Stone Brown, "Julian Bond: Leading the Movement into the Millennium," *The New Crisis*, January/February 2000, vol. 107, no. 1.

7. Taped author interview with Julian Bond, December 1999.

8. Mark Sherman, "New NAACP Concentrates on the Basics: Members at Atlanta Convention Urged to Fight Bias, Not Each Other," *The Atlanta Journal-Constitution*, July 12, 1998.

9. Hilary L. Hurd, "A Bonding Force," *Emerge*, May 1998, p. 38.

10. Mark Sherman, "Julian Bond's Great Expectations: The Once and Always Atlantan Takes the Helm of the NAACP and Returns to the Spotlight," *The Atlanta Journal-Constitution*, March 1, 1998.

11. Paul Shepard, "Controversy Dogs New NAACP Leader," *Associated Press Online*, March 4, 1998.

12. Claudia Dreifus, "Julian Bond: National Association for the Advancement of Colored People Chairman, Julian Bond Interview," *The Progressive*, August 1, 1998.

13. Ibid.

14. Fund-raising letter sent by the NAACP, April 2000, Julian Bond, Chairman of the Board, p. 4.

Chapter 11. Race Man

1. Lee May, "Julian Bond: At Home with Himself," *The Atlanta Journal-Constitution*, March 20, 1994, p. M-01.

2. Taped author interview with Julian Bond, February 2000.

3. Ibid.

4. Ibid.

5. Mark Sherman, "Julian Bond's Great Expectations: The Once and Always Atlantan Takes the Helm of the NAACP and Returns to the Spotlight," *The Atlanta Journal-Constitution*, March 1, 1998.

6. Keith L. Thomas, "Remembering the Dream: Julian Bond: Eyes on the Future," *The Atlanta Journal-Constitution*, January 15, 1990, p. E-01.

7. *Campaign and Campus News*, a newsletter of George School, Newtown, Pennsylvania ,1997.

8. Taped author interview with Julian Bond, December 1999.

FURTHER READING

Bond, Julian. *A Time to Speak, A Time to Act*. New York: Simon & Schuster, 1972.

Brinkley, Douglas. "Places at the Heart of the Movement." *American Legacy*, Summer 1997.

Brown, C. Stone. "NAACP Chairman Julian Bond: Still Spearheading the Cause of Racial Justice." *The New Crisis*, January/February 2000.

Dreifus, Claudia. "Julian Bond Interview." *The Progressive*, August 1, 1998.

Harris, Jacqueline. *The History and Achievement of the NAACP*. Danbury, Conn.: Franklin Watts, 1992.

Hurd, Hilary L. "A Bonding Force." *Emerge*, May 1998.

May, Lee. "Julian Bond, At Home with Himself: Teacher, Speaker and Activist Relish Both His Storied Past, Ordinary Riches of His Life." *The Atlanta Journal-Constitution*, March 20, 1994.

Neary, John. *Julian Bond, Black Rebel*. New York: William Morrow and Company, Inc., 1971.

Oliver, Stephanie Stokes. "The Private Side of Julian Bond." *Essence*, November 1983.

Williams, Roger M. *The Bonds: An American Family*. New York: Atheneum, 1972.

INTERNET ADDRESSES

Southern Poverty Law Center's
Julian Bond biography
<http://www.splcenter.org/centerinfo/julian.html>

The official site of the NAACP
<http://www.naacp.org/about/bond.html>

Type "Julian Bond" into the Site Search box for lots
of articles about Bond and about the NAACP
<http://www.africana.com>

"Activist Julian Bond Selected as NAACP
Chairman," CNN article
<http://www.cnn.com/us/9802/21/bond.naacp>

INDEX

Page numbers for photos are in **boldface** type.